The Householder's Electrical Guide

Geoffrey Burdett

Revised by Colin D. Kinloch DFH, CEng, MIEE

STANLEY PAUL

London Melbourne Auckland Johannesburg

Stanley Paul & Co. Ltd
An imprint of Century Hutchinson Ltd
62–65 Chandos Place, London WC2N 4NW

Century Hutchinson Australia (Pty) Ltd
PO Box 496, 16–22 Church Street, Hawthorn, Victoria 3122

Century Hutchinson New Zealand Ltd
PO Box 40–086, Glenfield, Auckland 10

Century Hutchinson South Africa (Pty) Ltd
PO Box 337, Bergvlei 2012, South Africa

First published 1973
Reprinted 1976, 1978, 1982, 1987

Set in Sabon

Printed and bound in Great Britain
by Anchor Brendon Ltd, Tiptree, Essex

ISBN 0 09 173462 2

Contents

Acknowledgements

The author acknowledges with thanks the assistance given by John O'Mahoney, Lecturer in Charge of Electrical Installation Work at the Harrow College of Technology and Art, for his helpful suggestions, reading the manuscript and checking proofs.

Illustrations

Line drawings

Photographs

Preface

When it comes to home improvements more and more people are becoming 'do-it-yourself' orientated. For there is much personal satisfaction to be gained from fixing or building something yourself, apart from the obvious financial saving when no contractor's bills have to be met.

This book has been written to give the practical householder and the mechanically minded housewife basic information about the domestic electrical installation. No puzzling formulae have been used; the work is entirely practical, ranging from replacing a blown fuse to installing an electric storage heater. And the emphasis is always on safety, because all information given conforms strictly to the official wiring regulations.

There is a lot of other useful information too: about how to get the electricity supply put on when moving house; what tariff to choose; how to read a meter and how to instruct an electrical contractor, should one need to be called in for jobs outside the householder's capabilities.

Electrical work is slightly different from other jobs which the householder might undertake because it does involve a high standard of proficiency for it to be completely safe. Every householder should know as much as possible about the source of power and light with which he constantly lives, and be capable of altering or fixing it when it becomes necessary.

The young man entering the electrical contracting industry, the shop assistant who needs to answer many questions from customers and the young woman embarking on a career as an Electrical Housecraft Adviser will all find this book an up-to-date and comprehensive source of facts.

In writing *The Householder's Electrical Guide*, Geoffrey Burdett has drawn on many years' experience in the electricity supply and electrical contracting industries as a professional, and from answering many thousands of questions asked by his magazine readers over a period of nearly twenty years. It follows, therefore, that you will find an answer to most of your problems by consulting this book.

While every effort has been made to ensure the accuracy of the information in this book, no responsibility can be accepted for any omission or for any misuse of the information given. For the full requirements for electrical installations, reference should be made to the Regulations for Electrical Installations published by the Institution of Electrical Engineers.

I

The Home Electrical Installation

Before the sixteenth century it was known that certain substances under friction, such as amber, would produce enough energy or static electricity to attract lightweight objects. But it took another two hundred years of scientific research before this natural phenomenon was tapped successfully and generated for practical use. From the discovery in 1802 that an electric spark, when struck between two carbon electrodes, emitted a brilliant light—the arc lamp—we are now able to flick a switch and produce the same effect. Today the trend is towards 'all-electric' homes, and it only takes a power cut for us to realise just how much we depend on this silent force to provide our basic needs; to light our way, keep us warm, cook our food and motivate all those labour-saving appliances which have become necessities in our lives.

It must be appreciated that electricity, in common with all forms of energy, is potentially dangerous, but the risks can be reduced to a minimum by observing the safety rules embodied in the Regulations for Electrical Installations published by the Institution of Electrical Engineers and commonly known as the IEE Wiring Regulations.

These Regulations are of a fairly complicated technical nature and include requirements for electrical installations in all kinds of premises from the smallest house to the largest factory or office block. This book explains the requirements for installations in houses.

To better understand domestic electrical applications we should first look at the source of power which, for the householder, is that mysterious and complicated set of wires, fuses and meters usually secreted beneath the stairs or in some equally dark and inaccessible place.

Consumer units

The home electrical installation consists of a number of individual circuits of various current ratings which radiate from a centrally situated position, usually adjacent to the Electricity Board's meter and fuse box. In modern or modernised installations these circuits are distributed from a consumer unit containing the necessary main switch plus all the fuses or miniature circuit breakers (MCBs). In older installations circuits are supplied from a number of main switch and fuse units of various types and current ratings. (These should be replaced by a modern consumer unit as soon as practicable.)

A house equipped with electric storage heating usually has a second consumer unit to supply these circuits or a single consumer unit with two groups of fuses or MCBs. This is necessary because storage heating circuits are time controlled to operate only during cheap night rate periods.

A consumer unit contains a number of fuses or MCBs of different current ratings (often referred to as 'ways')—one for

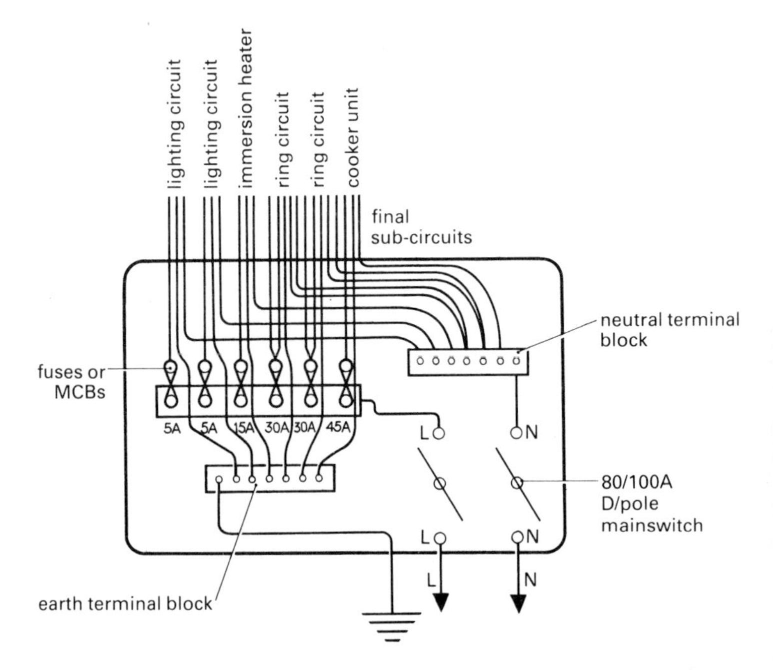

Fig. 1 Circuit wiring connections in a 6-way consumer unit

each circuit—and sometimes spare ways which are blanked off for future extensions to the installation. (When fitting a new unit at least one such spare way should be included.) Old type switch and fuse units, and some older fuse boards, have two fuses for each circuit: one for the phase and one for the neutral. It is now obligatory to have only one fuse per circuit (single-pole fusing), as double-pole fusing is potentially dangerous.

Consumer units are made in a wide range of sizes from 2-way to 10-way, which is the largest likely to be required for domestic use. There are also 1-way units consisting of a main switch and fuse unit in the one casing. Usually termed *switch-fuse units*, these have current ratings of 5A to 30A and higher, and are used for supplying single circuits. One version can be fitted with a fuse unit of any of four current ratings from 5A to 30A.

Multi-way units are usually fitted with fuses or MCBs of mixed rating to suit all the different circuits of the home installation; some units will also accommodate RCCBs. The current rating of the double-pole main switch varies with the size of the unit; 2-way units usually have a 45A main switch, larger sizes a 60A main switch, and the largest of all have an 80A or a 100A main switch. The tendency now is towards higher ratings to meet increasing load demands.

Standard current ratings of consumer unit fuses and MCBs are 5A, 15A, 20A and 30A. In addition, 45A cartridge fuses and 40, 45 or 50A MCBs are available for cooker and shower heater circuits. Although these various fuses and MCBs can be placed in any order in a consumer unit it is usual to fit those of highest rating next to the main switch and the lowest ones farthest away.

All the fuses are colour coded according to their current rating which makes it easier to select the correct fuse and also to locate the one which has 'blown'.

Fuses and MCBs are described on pp. 15ff and RCCBs on p. 27.

Large houses

For larger installations requiring a current over 100A, the installation is controlled by a main switch of appropriate current rating supplying two or more consumer units or other types of distribution board containing fuses or MCBs, located at suitable points in the building so as to reduce the length of the final circuits. Such installations must be properly designed to ensure safety and economy and are thus outside the scope of the ordinary householder.

Older fuse boards usually have fuses of one rating, which means that separate systems were required for lighting and power. However, the modern fuse board has fuses of mixed current rating and covers all circuits, as does the consumer unit.

Electricity Board's service fuse and meter

The supply of electricity comes into the house via a mains service cable run either underground or overhead, and its size is determined by the load demand of all appliances and lighting. The cable terminates in a sealed *terminal box* containing the *service fuse*, which is rated at 60A, 80A or 100A according to the assumed current demand of the installation. The terminal box normally contains only one fuse, which is in the line or phase conductor. Being larger than the fuses of the installation, it is least likely to blow in the event of a fault or overload. Should this occur, however, it is necessary to send for the Electricity Board, because only its engineers may break the seals to replace a service fuse.

The Board's distribution system consists of three lines or phases colour coded red, yellow and blue plus the neutral. Houses are supplied from any one of the three phases, and the colour is usually indicated by a disc on the apparatus. A house which takes above average load may be supplied from more than one phase, and the terminal box then contains one fuse for each to effect a load balance.

As the voltage between phases is 415V, a warning of this is given by a label on the main switch to avoid mistakes by the householder or his contractor.

2

Overcurrent Devices

Every circuit is designed to carry safely the maximum current required by the lights or appliances connected to it, but if this safe current were to be exceeded, resulting in an *overcurrent*, the conductors would overheat, damaging the insulation and giving rise to a risk of fire.

To prevent these harmful effects, every circuit must have an appropriate fuse or MCB which reacts to the overcurrent and automatically disconnects the circuit from the supply, thus acting as an intentional 'weak link'.

There are two levels of overcurrent which have to be prevented, namely *overload* and *short circuit*.

An overload usually occurs when too many lights or appliances or an over-large appliance is connected to a circuit giving a relatively small increase in current and therefore slow operation of the fuse or MCB. A short circuit occurs when phase and neutral conductors touch, giving a large increase in current and rapid operation of the fuse or MCB. These conditions are illustrated in Figs. 2 and 3.

Fuses and MCBs may also be used to interrupt large currents due to earth faults as illustrated in Fig. 4 and described in Chapter 3.

The fuse

Fuses of different sizes and ratings are fitted in consumer units, fuse boards, switch-fuse units, fused connection units and 13A plugs. Every fuse has three principal components:

a a fuse link—wire or cartridge
b a fuse holder
c a fuse base or shield.

The fuse wire or cartridge is housed in the fuse holder, which

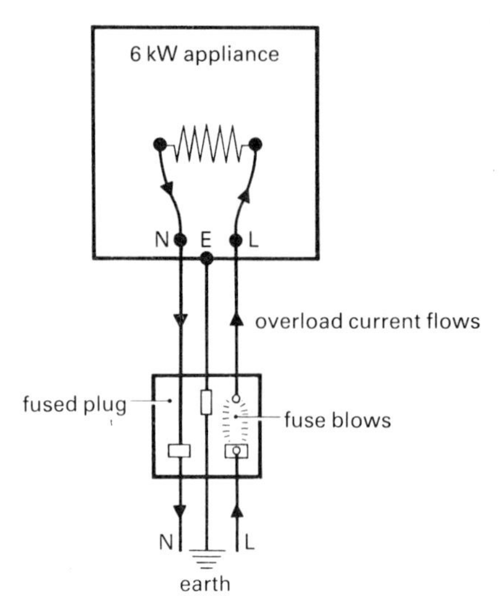

Fig. 2 Overload

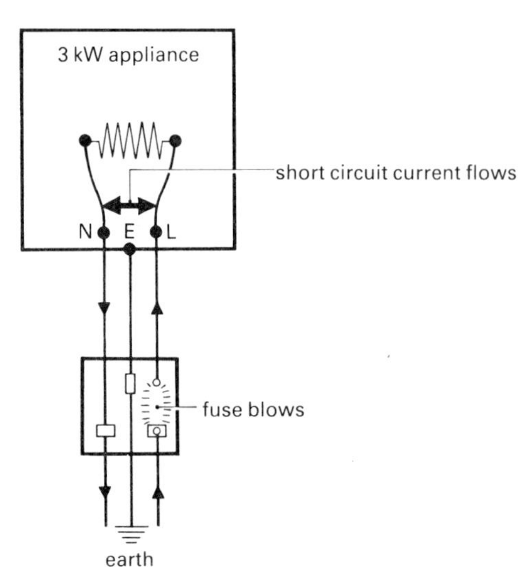

Fig. 3 Short circuit

is plugged into the fuse base containing the contacts connected to the circuit cables.

Types

There are two principal types of circuit fuses used in the home installation:

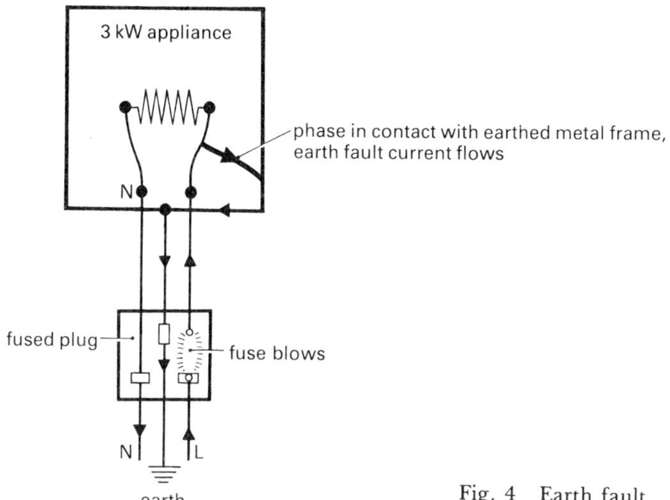

Fig. 4 Earth fault

a semi-enclosed (rewirable) fuses
b cartridge fuses.

Both have similar and sometimes identical bases and a similar holder. The fuse wire of the rewirable type is partially enclosed in an asbestos tube and secured to the contacts by milled nuts or screws; the cartridge fuse is either secured by a plastic or metal clamp or is contained in a tightly fitting plastic tube which forms part of the fuse holder moulding. Of the two, the cartridge fuse is superior, but it has disadvantages. The majority of fuses used in the home are of the rewirable type which use fuse wire of tinned copper. Sizes and ratings are given in Table 1.

Rewirable fuses

Advantages: They are cheap to replace: it is only necessary to have a card of the various wire ratings at hand to mend a fuse when it blows. A blown fuse can readily be seen by physical inspection when the fuse holder is withdrawn from the consumer unit.

Disadvantages: (i) It is not easy to renew, especially in the dark.

(ii) Fuse wire deteriorates in use, especially when the current in the circuit exceeds that of the fuse rating. The wire then runs hot, which erodes the coating of tin and copper, causing further overheating with the result that the fuse blows suddenly for no apparent reason (although a fault is suspected).

(iii) It is easily and therefore frequently abused. Larger fuse wire than necessary is inserted in the fuse holder in order to increase the load on the circuit or in an attempt to prevent a fuse blowing when there is a fault. The result is that the circuit cable becomes overloaded and is a potential fire risk. Hair pins and other objects which are sometimes used are an even greater hazard.

Table 1 *Rewirable Fuses*

Current rating of fuse	*Nominal diameter of wire*	*Circuit*
amps	*mm*	
5	0.20	Lighting
15	0.50	Immersion heater
20	0.60	Radial including storage heaters
30	0.85	Ring circuit and 30A radial
45	1.25	Cooker

Fuses are sometimes uprated inadvertently because the householder is unaware of the correct rating, but colour coding has been introduced to reduce the incidence of this. (Smaller fuse wire than the rating is not dangerous but leads to early deterioration, as indicated in (ii) above.)

(iv) A rewirable fuse carries up to twice the current of the fuse wire rating without blowing. For example over 60 amps is needed to blow a 30A fuse.

(v) It does not have sufficient breaking capacity to permit its use in all locations.

Cartridge fuses

A cartridge fuse link consists of a special wire element contained in a cartridge filled with quartz particles (sand) or other mineral to quench the arc when the fuse blows. The ends of the element are secured to metal end caps which make the electrical contact with the fuse holder.

Advantages: (i) A blown fuse is easily replaced by a new one of the same current rating.

(ii) The physical size of the cartridge varies with the current rating of the fuse; the higher the current rating, the larger the cartridge. It is therefore impossible to fit a 20A fuse or a 30A fuse into a 5A fuse holder, either intentionally or by mistake.

(iii) Less overcurrent is needed to blow a cartridge fuse than a rewirable fuse, and it therefore affords greater protection to the circuit. A cartridge fuse carries up to 1½ times its current rating. For example, it needs over 45 amps to blow a 30A fuse, compared to over 60 amps for a rewirable type.

(iv) The breaking capacity is adequate for any house installation.

Disadvantages: (i) Replacement costs are high, especially when a fuse blows repeatedly because the fault has not been located.

(ii) Spare fuses of each rating have to be kept at hand.

(iii) Where no spare fuse is available there is a temptation to use fuse wire or some metallic object as a substitute. This is a dangerous practice, for such 'fuses' can disintegrate on blowing and cause substantial damage.

(iv) It is not possible by visual inspection to tell when a cartridge fuse has blown.

Cartridge fuse ratings are distinguished by their colour and also by the current rating stamped on them. Those which are also stamped BS1361 have the following colours: 5A white; 15A blue; 20A yellow; 30A red and 45A green; spots of the same colour appear on the face of the holders. Holders of rewirable fuses are similarly coded. Plastic fuse holders are coloured.

Plug fuses

These are cartridge fuses of similar high standard as circuit fuses. They are colour coded thus: 3A, red; 13A, brown; all other ratings, black. (The 3A fuse was previously coloured blue.)

What to do when a fuse blows

When a circuit fuse blows, extinguishing the lights in part of the house or cutting off the supply to sockets or fixed appliances, you should be able to go into the meter cupboard and, with the aid of a torch, turn off the main switch, open the consumer unit cover and read on the inside which fuse supplies that circuit. If you have not listed the circuits you will have to withdraw each fuse until you find the one which has blown. If the lighting circuit has failed, try the 5A fuses with their white colour coding. Examine each fuse in turn until you come to one with broken wire (though if a short circuit is the cause the wire may have disintegrated). If it is a cartridge fuse, first check that you have a spare. If necessary test it, for it may be a dud. As you withdraw each fuse close the lid of the consumer unit and turn on the main switch to check if you have located the right circuit.

Having found it, you should first try to ascertain what caused the fuse to blow. If this happened immediately you switched on one of the lights and was accompanied by a slight bang or loud 'plop', it was probably a faulty flex. In either case you should turn off the switch and remove the bulb. If the fuse blew without anything being switched on at that moment and there was no 'plop', the cause was probably fuse wire deterioration, to which reference has already been made.

An iron, kettle or drill plugged into a light socket will also cause a fuse to blow. So will a heat/light unit. A ring circuit fuse will blow only through very serious overloading or because of a fault in the wiring: faulty appliances blow the individual plug fuse, not the circuit fuse.

Having located the fault, you can now deal with the fuse. First you should turn off the main switch, not because it is dangerous to replace a fuse with the mains on, but should there be a fault in the circuit the ensuing 'bang' when the new fuse is inserted will be less frightening.

Successive blowing of a fuse indicates a serious fault, probably in the wiring, which will need the services of an electrician. Recall whether you have recently driven nails in floorboards or drilled a wall so that you may have pierced a cable.

Mending fuses

The sequence for repairing a fuse is as follows. First, turn off the main switch:

Rewirable fuse

Locate 'blown' fuse and remove from consumer unit or fuse board.

Try to locate and correct the fault which caused the fuse to blow.

Remove old fuse wire from the fuse holder.

Insert new fuse wire of correct current rating in the porcelain of the fuse holder. Tighten screws and trim ends of wire but be careful not to stretch the wire too tightly when tightening the second screw.

Replace fuse holder in fuseway. Switch on to test the circuit.

Cartridge fuse

Locate blown fuse and remove holder from consumer unit.

Try to locate and correct fault which caused the fuse to blow.

Remove cartridge from fuse holder.

Check that fuse has blown and discard cartridge.

Insert new cartridge of correct current rating into fuse holder.

Replace fuse holder in fuseway of consumer unit. Switch on to test the circuit.

Plug fuses

Remove cap of plug.

Prise out old fuse and discard it.

Select new fuse of appropriate current rating, first checking that the existing fuse was correct: 3A red (formerly blue) for appliances up to 700W including table lamps and floor standards: 13A brown for appliances between 700W and 3000W.

Insert the fuse in the plug. Check that it is secure and makes good electrical contact.

Replace plug cap and test in socket.

Fused connection units

These, also termed *fused spur boxes*, contain a fuse identical in size and current ratings to that of plug fuses. It is removed by prising out the anchored fuse holder on the front of the unit which allows the fuse to fall out. With some types the fuse holder is detachable and is removed by releasing a screw.

Fit in the new fuse and replace the cover using the reverse sequence.

Miniature circuit breakers

A miniature circuit breaker (MCB) is a single-pole switch which automatically switches itself off when overcurrent flows through its operating coil and therefore in a circuit. It is a superior alternative to a fuse and its only significant disadvantage is its higher initial cost, but time and money otherwise spent in replacing fuses can be saved.

Current ratings are similar to those for circuit fuses. Consumer units and fuse boards are made which will take either fuses or MCBs but, in the main, consumer units are designed specifically for one or the other. In common with fuse-type consumer units, MCBs of the various current ratings are interchangeable, enabling any mixture of ratings to be assembled to suit the installation.

The principal advantage of the MCB from the safety aspect is that its characteristics are preset by the manufacturer and can only be altered by replacing the MCB by one of a different rating, thus avoiding the risk associated with fitting an incorrect fuse wire. There is no need to have spare fuse links as it is only necessary to turn the MCB on again after repair of the fault which caused it to trip.

The manually operated dolly or push-button on the MCB enables a circuit to be switched on and off without affecting other circuits. With some models this is a 3-position switch. In addition to 'Up' and 'Down' the switch dolly has a mid-way position which it returns to when tripped by a circuit fault or overload. This enables the householder to see at a glance whether the switch has been turned off manually or has tripped out because of a fault.

One make of MCB uses press-buttons instead of a switch. These are plug-in types fitted in the Wylex range of consumer units and fuse boards, and they are interchangeable with fuses—either rewirable or cartridge—and can be fitted to an existing unit by removing the fuse and changing the fuse base if the existing fuses are rewirable. A section of the consumer unit cover has also to be 'knocked-out' to accommodate the MCBs and to give access to manual switching. Circuit details are written on a label on the face of the MCB, the press-button gives the current rating and the units are colour coded as for circuit fuses.

It is important to say at this stage that an MCB must not be confused with a residual current circuit breaker (RCCB). An MCB is an overcurrent device which is alternative to a fuse. An RCCB, as is shown later, is a method of affording effective earthing arrangement and does not usually provide any overcurrent protection. Some patterns of RCCB do, however, incorporate overcurrent protection.

3
Electric Shock

The principal hazard associated with the use of electricity is electric shock, which results when a current flows through part of a human (or animal) body. A large part of the IEE Wiring Regulations is devoted to preventing this hazard.

The severity of a shock depends on the magnitude of the shock current, its duration and the path taken by the current through the body. If the current flows near the heart, as may occur when the shock is sustained from hand to hand or hand to foot, a current as low as 10mA may be fatal unless it is interrupted quickly. Conversely, a larger current entering and leaving at, say, two points on a finger is unlikely to be fatal but may cause severe burning as well as a risk of secondary injury due to involuntary movement.

The magnitude of the shock current depends mainly on the voltage between the points of contact and the resistance of the skin. When the skin is moist with perspiration or from immersion in water, its resistance decreases and the shock current increases. For this reason, special rules apply to electrical equipment in bathrooms (see pp. 45, 49, 134–5).

Direct and indirect contact

These terms describe the two ways in which electric shock can occur.

Direct contact refers to the shock risk resulting from touching two exposed live parts at different voltages or touching one exposed live part and other metalwork which is in contact with earth. Protection against direct contact is afforded by: durable insulation covering live parts so as to prevent contact therewith (for example, the insulation on a cable); and enclosure of live

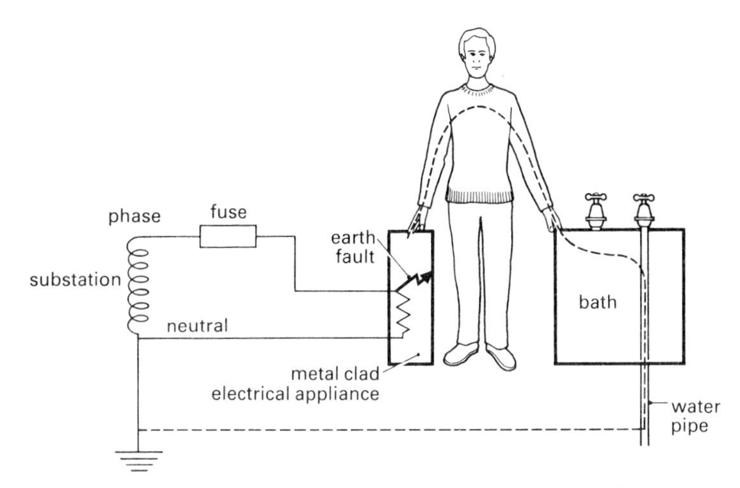

Fig. 5 Indirect contact shock risk—'hand to hand shock'

parts in a robust metal or plastics box (for example, a socket box or the casing of a consumer unit).

Indirect contact refers to the shock risk resulting from touching an exposed conductive part (for example, the metal casing of an item of electrical equipment) which has become live as a result of a fault within the equipment or elsewhere in the installation.

For instance, if there is failure of insulation, a live part might touch the casing, making it live at 240V; if a person were to touch simultaneously the exposed conductive part and other earthed metalwork such as a metal water pipe, a current would flow through the body as shown in Fig. 5.

To protect against indirect contact, three things are required:

(**a**) earthing of exposed conductive parts
(**b**) automatic disconnection of the supply in the event of an earth fault
(**c**) electrical bonding of exposed conductive parts to simultaneously accessible extraneous conductive parts (i.e. earthed metalwork).

Automatic disconnection by fuses or MCBs

For fuses or MCBs to be effective for shock protection, the earthing of exposed conductive parts must ensure that enough

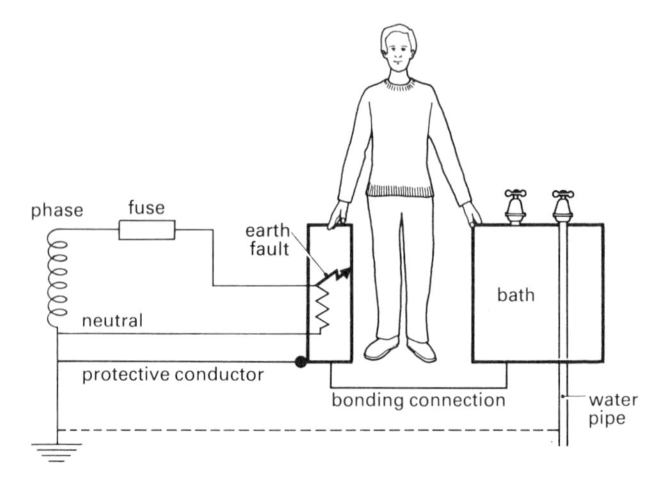

Fig. 6 Indirect contact shock risk reduced by earthing and bonding

earth fault current flows so as to cause the fuse or MCB to operate within 5 seconds or 0.4 second, according to the type of circuit. At the same time, bonding brings all simultaneously accessible metalwork to substantially the same voltage. This is shown in Fig. 6. When an earth fault occurs, a large current flows in the phase (L) conductor causing the fuse or MCB to operate. During the time that this takes, the major part of the earth fault current flows to earth via the bonding conductor and the pipe, but the presence of the bonding means that only a negligible current flows through the body of the person in contact with the two conductive parts.

Disconnection time

As stated above, disconnection must occur within 5 seconds or 0.4 second after the occurrence of an earth fault, according to the type of circuit as follows:

lighting circuit	5 seconds
lighting circuit feeding bathroom	0.4 second
socket outlet circuit (including ring circuit)	0.4 second
cooker circuit (no socket in cooker unit)	5 seconds

cooker circuit (with socket in cooker unit)	0.4 second
storage heater circuit	5 seconds
shower heater circuit	0.4 second

The disconnection time achieved in practice depends on the magnitude of the earth fault current and hence on the earth loop impedance at the point of fault. The maximum circuit lengths given in Table 4 on p. 71 take account of this requirement.

Automatic disconnection by RCCB

Where the earthing arrangements do not allow the flow of enough fault current to operate fuses or MCBs within the specified time, it is necessary to install one or more residual current circuit breakers (RCCBs) and an earth electrode consisting of a metal rod driven into the ground immediately outside the house.

An RCCB was previously known as a current-operated earth leakage circuit breaker. When an earth fault occurs, the currents in the phase and neutral conductors are no longer equal because the fault current in the phase conductor returns via the circuit protective conductor; the RCCB detects this difference in the phase and neutral currents (referred to as the *residual current*) and the switching mechanism operates to disconnect the circuit or installation from the supply, usually within 0.2 second.

An RCCB may serve as the main switch for an installation, in which case it will be suitable for a load current of 60A or 100A and will have an operating current of 100mA to 500mA. Other RCCBs are suitable for shock protection in individual circuits, for which purpose an operating current of 30mA is usually selected. Both types may be incorporated in modern consumer units or installed separately.

Voltage-operated earth leakage circuit breakers

These devices are installed on many older installations where the Electricity Board was unable to offer earthing facilities. They are now considered obsolete and should no longer be relied on for automatic disconnection in the event of an earth fault. It is possible that the Electricity Board can now provide an earthing terminal but, if not, the voltage-operated device should be replaced by an RCCB.

Earthing

To ensure satisfactory automatic disconnection in the event of an earth fault, whether by fuses, MCBs or RCCBs, correct earthing of exposed conductive parts is essential. To facilitate this, a circuit protective conductor (CPC) is required for every circuit for lighting, socket outlets and fixed appliances and in flexible cords to portable appliances. One end of the CPC is connected to the earthing terminal of the wiring accessory or appliance and the other end to the main earthing terminal in the consumer unit or, for old installations, to a separate earthing terminal adjacent to the main switch.

From the main earthing terminal, an earthing conductor (16 sq. mm) runs to the actual means of earthing, which may be an earthing terminal provided by the Electricity Board or, where this is not available, an earth electrode outside the house.

Water pipes are no longer acceptable as means of earthing because of the introduction of plastics pipes. If the Electricity Board cannot provide an earthing terminal, an RCCB and earth rod should be installed without delay where the existing earthing arrangements depend on a water pipe.

Bonding

To establish a zone of substantially uniform voltage on accessible metalwork within a building, effective bonding must be provided between exposed conductive parts and other earthed metalwork. Main bonding conductors of 10 sq. mm copper are run from the main earthing terminal to any metal pipes bringing water, gas or oil into the house. Connection to these pipes is made by clamps complying with BS 951 as near as practicable to the point of entry, except that the connection to gas pipes should be made on the consumer's side of the gas meter.

Provided that the pipework is electrically continuous throughout the building, no additional bonding is required except in bathrooms. However, the use of plastics tanks and fittings is now common, so that it may be necessary to provide supplementary bonding conductors to lengths of pipework and other items which are not effectively bonded by the main bonding conductors.

In bathrooms and shower rooms, all exposed metalwork (baths, taps, radiators etc) should be bonded locally, using 4 sq. mm green and yellow cable, in addition to any bonding elsewhere. This does not imply the need to connect unsightly bonding conductors to each tap as they can usually be connected unobtrusively to the adjacent pipe, provided that it is then in effective electrical contact with the exposed metal tap.

Other methods of protection against indirect contact

All-insulated and double-insulated equipment

As the name implies, all-insulated equipment is constructed without any exposed conductive parts so that there is nothing to be earthed. Double-insulated equipment, on the other hand, does have exposed metalwork, but also incorporates an enhanced level of insulation to separate live parts from the metal casing with the result that earthing of the exposed metalwork is not required; such equipment is identified by the symbol ⧈ on the rating plate.

As no earthing is necessary, appliances of both types are fitted with two-core flexes without protective conductors; the brown and blue cores are connected to the 'L' and 'N' terminals of the plug and no connection is made to the 'E' terminal.

Electrical separation

This method of protection against indirect contact requires the use of a special isolating transformer to afford separation of an appliance or other equipment from earth. The usual example found in homes is the shaver socket unit to BS 3052 for use in bathrooms (see p. 134).

4

Flexible Cords

A flexible cord is an electric cable with either one, two or three insulated conductors known as *cores*, each consisting of numerous strands. The small flex used in the home installation has 16-strand conductors; the largest has conductors of 65 strands. It is these strands which provide the cable's necessary flexibility.

Most flexible cords now have an overall insulated sheathing to provide extra mechanical protection to the insulated cores, but some older twin-core flex as well as single-core flex is non-sheathed.

Four types or classes of flexible cords are used in homes, depending on the application and the situation. These are:

(i) *Braided circular flex*, made in both 2-core and 3-core versions and with a 2-colour braiding. Cotton fillers provide the circular cross-section. It is fitted to a wide variety of domestic electrical appliances including portable electric fires, but is confined to dry situations indoors. Cores are usually rubber insulated.

(ii) *Unkinkable flex* .3-core rubber insulated flex has a light rubber sheathing in which is partially embedded a 2-colour braid. It is fitted to electric irons and kettles.

(iii) *Circular sheathed flex* is made in 2-core and 3-core versions with either a rubber or a pvc sheath. This is a general purpose flexible cord for inside and outside use and is fitted to vacuum cleaners, floor polishers, electric drills and a variety of portable electric tools where a long lead is required. Extension flexible cords, often contained on drums fitted with a socket-outlet, are of this type too. Sheath colours are grey or black for general purpose use, bright orange or yellow for hedge trimmers, mowers and other gardening tools, and white (but sometimes black) for pendant light fittings when it is used instead of twisted twin flex. When cable is used from a drum always unroll the cable from the drum, or it may overheat. Heat resistant circular flex insulated in butyl rubber of various compounds is made for connection to immersion heaters and other heaters where there is high temperature within the terminal box.

(iv) *Flat twin sheathed flex* is a version of parallel twin flex with pvc insulation and sheathing. It is fitted to some double-insulated, and all-insulated appliances where sheathing is necessary to prevent the abrasion of the core insulation, and colour coding of the cores is desirable.

Core colours

Since 1970 it has been a statutory requirement that every earthed portable domestic electrical appliance and every earthed light fitting be wired with 3-core flex of standard colours. A shop selling either new or second-hand appliances and fittings with flex in any other colours is committing an offence.

The new colours are: *brown* (phase); *blue* (neutral); and striped *green/yellow* (earth). These replace the former flex core colours which were standard in Britain: red (phase); black (neutral); and green (earth). Flexible cords in other countries had cores of various colours, but these are now the same as those here.

The statutory requirement does not extend to 2-core flex, for this is only fitted to appliances and light fittings which do not require an earth connection (e.g. double-insulated appliances). Nevertheless, two-core sheathed flex is now made with the new core colours of brown for the 'live' core and blue for the neutral. The cores of pvc twisted twin and parallel twin flex are one colour or transparent. One core is sometimes distinguished by ribbing along its length, but as that is not always so, this type of flex cannot be used where the lamp or appliance is controlled by a single-pole cord switch or built-in switch or a thermostat, which must be connected to the live pole.

Flex sizes

Flexible cord used in the home is made in a number of sizes having a range of current ratings from 3A to 25A. The number and diameter of strands differ with the current rating. All are in metric sizes, as shown in Table 2.

Table 2 *Flexible Cords*

Size	*Current rating*	*Maximum weight supportable by twin flex*	*Application*
mm²	*amps*	*kg (lb)*	
0.5	3	2 (4)	Lighting fittings
0.75	6	3 (6)	Lighting fittings and small appliances
1.0	10	5 (10)	Appliances up to 2400 watts
1.5	15	5 (10)	Appliances up to 3600 watts
2.5	20	5 (10)	Appliances up to 4800 watts
4	25	5 (10)	Appliances up to 6000 watts

Renewing a flex

When a flexible cord on an appliance is renewed, it will almost certainly be fitted with the old type flex. As the new flex will be in the new colour coding it is important to remember both the old and the new colours so that you connect it correctly. If it is an imported appliance and the flex cores are entirely different colours from those in Britain, make sure you know which are the different terminals and do not hesitate to have the appliance checked at the shop where you buy the new flex.

Extending flex

A flexible cord must not be lengthened by twisting the ends and wrapping the joint in insulation tape. Any joint must be mechanically strong as well as electrically sound, and this is only possible when a proper flex connector is used. Generally, it is better to discard the flex and fit a new length. The exception is a power tool lead or other long circular sheathed flex for which extension leads are available, as an alternative.

There are two types of connector: one is solid with fixed terminals and cord grips for anchoring the sheath. The conductors of the old and new flex must be of the correct polarity, which means they must be fitted into the correct terminals. The rule is: brown to red; blue to black; and green/yellow to green. Where both the existing and the extension flex are of the new colours cores of identical colours are, of course, inserted in the terminals.

The other type of connector is a two-piece 'plug-and-socket' unit. The terminals are marked *L*, *N* and *E* in each section, so there should be no problem. It is, however, essential for the plug portion of this connector to be fitted to the appliance side of the flex extension and for the socket portion to be connected to the mains side which is 'live' when the lead is plugged into the supply in the house socket-outlet. The socket (or female portion) is usually marked *MAINS* to avoid a wrong connection.

Connecting flex to a plug

A flexible cord must be connected correctly, as shown in the photographs for the standard 13A fused plug. The green/yellow (or green) earth core is the most important from the safety aspect and should be connected first to the large pin in the centre top. The brown (or red) which is the phase and next important is connected to the terminal on the right and in contact with the fuse. The blue (or black) core, the neutral, is connected to the terminal on the left. Before fitting the plug cover ensure that the flex sheath is well anchored in the sheath clamp so that there is no undue strain on the conductors when the flex is pulled.

Plugs of other sizes and types have various terminal arrangements and anchorage and should be carefully examined before the flex is renewed.

Plug adaptors

Plug adaptors are multi-outlet devices which enable more than one appliance to be run off a single socket-outlet. They should be used only where absolutely necessary to avoid numerous trailing flexes and the risk of overloading a socket.

Where plugs smaller than the main plug are used the adaptor should contain a fuse to protect the flex of lower current rating. *Some mixed rating adaptors do not have fuses, and these can be dangerous.*

Socket distribution units

These are a form of adaptor, but connected by a flexible cord to a parent plug. The total loading on the unit must not exceed the rated capacity of the socket supplying it. Some distribution units contain a fuse or circuit breaker to prevent overloading, and most have neon indicators. The units are particularly suitable for supplying small tools and portable lamps in the workshop and garage, and they have some use in the house; but they should not be regarded as a substitute for additional, permanently wired socket-outlets. Single sockets for connection to an extension lead are termed *trailing sockets*, and are of rubber or pvc construction.

5

Lamps and Lighting

The most commonly used electric lamp in the home is the ordinary light bulb. This has a tungsten wire filament enclosed in a gas-filled glass bulb and a brass bayonet (bc) lamp cap. The bulb is made in two principal forms: single-coil filament and coiled coil filament, which gives the greater light output for a given wattage.

The single-coil bc bulb is made in eight sizes from 15W to 200W. The coiled coil is made in four sizes: 40W, 60W, 100W, and 150W, which are the principal sizes used in the home. Since coiled coil lamps are more efficient and give more light than single coil they should be chosen in the available sizes (wattage).

Another relevant variation is the glass bulb or envelope itself. This can be plain or pearl and bulb or mushroom shaped. Mushroom shape bulbs all have coiled coil filaments. Pink pearl is another variant. These are mainly single-coil lamps, but some are mushroom shaped.

Pearl and pink pearl bulbs are used mainly in pendants and fittings where the lamp is exposed to the eyes. Clear bulbs, which are slightly more efficient, are preferred in enclosed and in

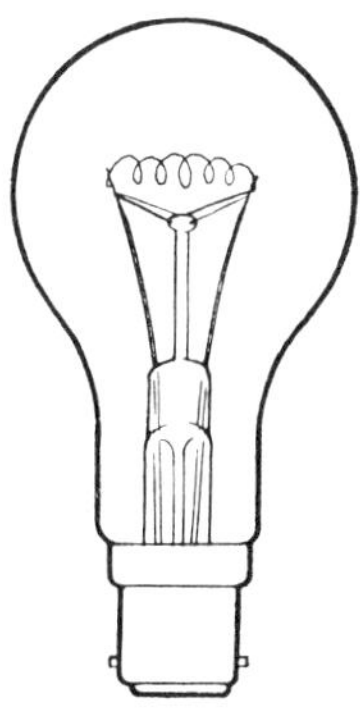

Fig. 7 Cut-away view of light bulb

decorative fittings. Bulbs in different colours are also available, and there are a number of special lamps of various shapes (such as 'Gala') used in fittings without shades. For wall lighting and some pendants, candle lamps can be used, which come in a range of shapes: olive plain and olive twisted, in clear, opal and pink pearl; frosted coloured; and small round bulbs of 15W and 20W. One candle bulb even incorporates a flickering wick.

Strip lights

Strip type lamps 9–12 in. (225–300 mm) long have a tungsten filament enclosed in a clear or frosted tubular glass envelope with single-contact lamp caps at each end. They come in 30W and 60W sizes, in white, frosted pink and amber colours and have numerous purposes in the home from picture lighting to illuminating the aquarium.

A more attractive version is the architectural tubular lamp, which can be either straight, in lengths from 12 to 48 in. (300–1200 mm) of 35–150 watts, or curved at 60 watts. All are opal, have single-pin caps for fitting into special lampholders and are fixed direct to the wall or ceiling.

Longer-life electric light bulbs

The ordinary electric light bulb has an average life of about 1000 hours. This is comparatively short because the bulbs are designed to produce the highest possible light output for a given wattage. It is possible to produce bulbs with a much longer life but only at the expense of light output. Such bulbs are now available, some of which have double the life of the ordinary bulb and others, an almost indefinite life.

They cost more to buy but are worth trying out, especially in fittings where you do not want to be replacing bulbs at fairly short intervals.

Fluorescent lighting

A fluorescent lamp is an electronic tube in various lengths and wattages, operated in conjunction with control gear consisting of starter switch, ballast (choke) and capacitor incorporated in the fluorescent luminaire (lighting fitting).

Some fluorescent luminaires have starterless control gear, but these are mainly used in industrial or commercial premises.

How a fluorescent tube operates

The tubular glass envelope is coated on the inside with a fluorescent powder and contains a small quantity of special gas. At each end is a cathode or electrode consisting of a wire filament or braided element which is connected to a bi-pin lamp cap.

When the lamp is switched on the electrodes are heated and a high-voltage current produced by the choke 'strikes' across the two cathodes and starts a flow of electrons along the tube. These electrons bombard the glass envelope, excite the fluorescent coating and produce the characteristic light. (Various tones or colours are obtained by mixing impurities with the fluorescent powder.)

The starter switch is a small 'make and break' device which is enclosed in a metal or plastic canister which has two contact pins for fitting into a starter holder on the fitting.

There is no pre-warming in the quick-start circuit, for there is no starter switch. The result is that some of the cathodes' coating is eroded each time the tube is switched on, so reducing the expected life of the lamp. Some such erosion occurs with switch start circuits too, but it is much less. Since, however, the expected life of a fluorescent tube is over 7000 hours (representing about ten years' use) a slightly shorter life can hardly be termed a financial problem. Nevertheless it is an economy to minimise the switch on and off frequency and therefore reduce the rate of erosion.

Fluorescent lighting is usually used where a good level of illumination is required for fairly long periods, for example in kitchens and utility rooms, but decorative luminaires are now available for living rooms. Packs containing tubes and luminaires are widely available, as are replacement tubes when needed.

Faults and their remedies concerning fluorescent tubes and fittings are detailed on p. 42–3.

Choosing the tube colour

Among the numerous tones or colours produced by fluorescent tubes are 'Coolwhite', 'White', 'Warmwhite', 'Warmwhite de Luxe' and various proprietory colours such as 'Softone', 'Kolor-rite' and many more.

The 'colour' must be suitable for the home, and the most widely used is Warmwhite de Luxe, which can be used in most fittings. Proprietory colours such as 'Softone' are also suitable for the home and are sold for that purpose in addition to other applications where a warm light is required.

Hitherto, fluorescent tubes have been 1½ in. (38 mm) in diameter and these are still available as replacements for existing luminaires. Recently introduced energy-saving tubes of 1 in. (26 mm) diameter can be used only in luminaires designed for them.

The principal advantage of fluorescent lighting is that it gives much more light than does the tungsten filament bulb of the same wattage.

For example: a 40W Warmwhite tube produces about 2800 lumens of light compared with under 400 lumens from a 40W coiled coil filament lamp. As, however, the choke of a fluorescent fitting also consumes electricity, allowance must be made for this when making current consumption comparisons.

A more realistic comparison is a 40W fluorescent Warmwhite tube, which produces 2800 lumens and a 60W coiled coil bulb, which produces 660 lumens. On that basis, allowing 20 watts for the choke, it can be said that a Warmwhite fluorescent tube provides four times the light of a tungsten filament lamp for the same electricity consumption. Coolwhite, White, and Warmwhite colour tubes all have a greater light output than Warmwhite de Luxe; other 'colours' produce less light, the lowest being Artificial Daylight with its 1200 lumens for a 40W tube.

Sizes and types of tubes

Among the extensive range of fluorescent tubes there are three principal sizes most suitable for the home: the 5 ft (1500 mm) 65W, the 4 ft (1200 mm) 40W, and the 2 ft (600 mm) 20W

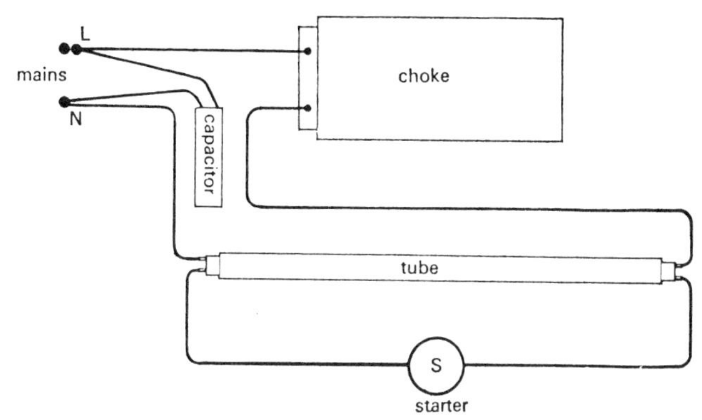

Fig. 8 Fluorescent tube circuits—a switch start single tube circuit

They are all available in 1½ in. and 1 in. in diameter, and are used in both single- and twin-tube fittings.

Where a twin-tube luminaire incorporates two independent circuits, the light output and electricity consumption can sometimes be reduced by removing one of the starter switches. However, some circuits require both tubes to operate simultaneously, and removal of one tube may even result in increased electricity consumption.

Circuit accessories

A starter switch, a choke and a capacitor are the accessories, and these vary with the type of circuit. The functions of choke and starter have already been explained. The capacitor is usually used for power factor correction and plays no significant part in the tube's operation. In some circuits, such as twin-tube series circuits, the capacitor performs a function, and no power factor correction is necessary.

Power factor correction capacitors are made in various sizes to suit the circuit, and any replacement must be identical to the original. They are required by the Electricity Board and any home constructed fluorescent fitting must include one, because the choke produces what is termed *wattless current*, which is not recorded or measured on the electricity meter. This 'lagging' current is expressed as a percentage, whereas tungsten filament lighting has what is termed unity power factor. A fluorescent

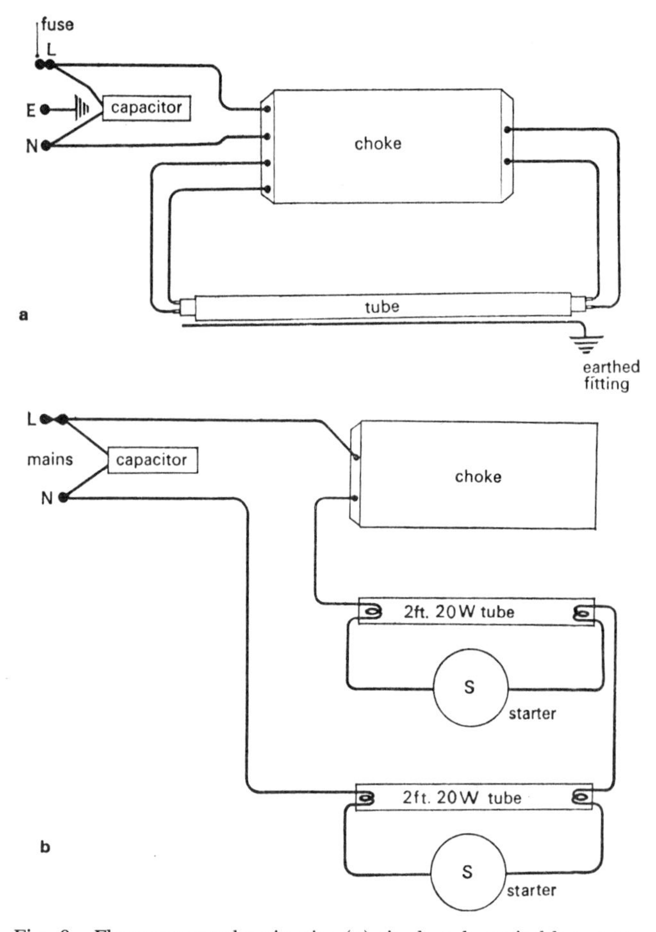

Fig. 9 Fluorescent tube circuits (a) single tube switchless start (b) twin-tube switch start circuit

choke reduces this to about 0.65 (lagging), and the Board requires it to be corrected or improved to at least 0.85 or 85% of unity, which is the function of the capacitor. Some circuits produce a leading power factor, in excess of unity, which is dealt with by other means.

Pelmet lighting using fluorescent tubes

Fluorescent tubes fixed behind the pelmet can be used quite effectively to illuminate the curtains when drawn. Batten-type luminaires, fixed to the pelmet board at a distance of 4–6 in. (200–300 mm) in front of the curtains will flood the whole of the curtain area with light. If set closer only the tops of the curtains are likely to be illuminated, but some experiment is usually necessary to get the optimum effect. The ends of the tube must extend a few inches beyond the width of the curtains, and if more than one tube is used to get the required length the joins must overlap to prevent 'breaks' or gaps in the overall light.

For downward lighting only, reflector tubes can be used, and these must be fitted the correct way so that the internal reflector is on top when the tube is in position. Upward light, reflected from the ceiling, requires a pelmet with an open top.

This and other types of supplementary lighting can be supplied from a spur off the ring circuit via a fused outlet, or from a lighting circuit. The switches can be local or remote as required.

Circular fluorescent fittings

These are fitted with circular tubes in diameters of: 8½ in. (200 mm) 22W; 12 in. (300 mm) 32W; and 18 in. (400 mm) 40W. Some fittings have two tubes of different diameters. The circuits are usually switch start types and include choke, starter switch and capacitor.

Miniature fluorescent tubes

'Mini-tubes' give high lumen output with low power consumption: roughly five times the light output of the equivalent in tungsten filament bulbs. In the home, their long life, low operating temperature and small size make them suitable for many situations where a bulb or filament strip light would normally be used: for instance embodied in the control panel of a cooker.

Sizes are: 6 in. (150 mm) 4W; 9 in. (225 mm) 6W; 12 in. (300 mm) 8W and 21 in. (450 mm) 13W. Tube diameter is 16 mm and the lamp caps are mini bi-pin.

Fault finding

Unlike a filament lamp, a fluorescent tube does not usually fail suddenly or completely. It normally shows some form of life, depending on the nature of the fault and whether it is in the

Table 3 *Fluorescent Tube Failures*

Tube behaviour	*Probable cause*
Tube appears completely dead.	Circuit fuse or fuse in fitting or plug blown; break in circuit wiring; or, if a switch-start circuit, a faulty lampholder contact or broken tube electrode.
Electrodes glow at each end, but tube makes no attempt to start.	*Switch-start type*: If glow is white, faulty starter; if red, tube is at end of useful life. *Switchless-start type*: Ineffective earth connection at metal fitting or to lamp caps.
Tube glows at one end only when trying unsuccessfully to start.	*Switch-start type*: Lampholder connection at dead end of tube short-circuited. *Switchless-start type*: Broken tube electrode or disconnection at dead end of tube.
Tube makes repeated but unsuccessful efforts to start.	Faulty starter; low mains voltage; tube is very old. Twin-tube circuit: lampholder connections crossed.
Tube lights normally for a few seconds, then goes out and repeats.	Faulty starter; low mains voltage; tube past its useful life, especially where it extinguishes with a shimmering effect.*
Tube lights up but at half brightness.	Tube past its useful life.
Series twin-tube circuit, i.e. two 20W 2 ft tubes: one tube extra bright, other tube not alight.	Starter faulty or is wrong type for the circuit.

*NB. A new tube sometimes lights with a shimmering effect. The tube is not faulty, but soon settles down to normal working.

tube or in a component. The behaviour of a tube with a fault is a good indication of the trouble.

Table 3 lists the more common faults and shows how they are diagnosed and rectified.

6

Space Heating

Heat emitted by an electric space heater is either radiant heat or convected heat. Radiant heat is usually associated with visible 'red' elements, but some panel heaters and storage radiators emit radiant heat from a 'black' surface. Convector heaters have elements usually operating at 'black' heat.

The principal difference between the two is that radiant heat is the passage of heat from places of high temperature to places or objects of lower temperature without raising the temperature of the intervening air, while convected heat is basically the production of warm air.

Although radiant electric heaters emit heat mainly by radiation and convectors mainly by convection, most radiant heaters emit some heat by convection and most convectors produce some radiant heat. The proportions depend on the particular design. Some electric heaters are designed as combined radiant/

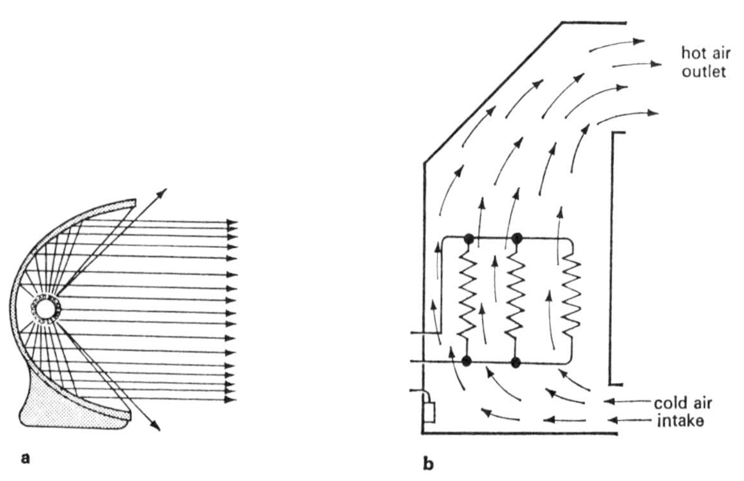

Fig. 10 Two forms of heat emission from electric fires
(a) radiant heat (b) convected heat

convector heaters, and they contain both types of elements which operate at 'red' heat and 'black' heat respectively.

The traditional radiant heater or electric fire with exposed elements operating at red heat is designed mainly to supply a large measure of localised heat for short periods; a convector is used for a more overall continuous heat. However, with the development of the low temperature panel heaters, skirting heaters and other 'low temperature' heaters which emit heat mainly by radiation, background heating is no longer confined to convectors.

Modern electric heaters are generally divided into two classes: direct-acting and storage.

Direct-acting heaters are so termed because they produce heat immediately they are switched on and cease to do so almost immediately after they are switched off. There are numerous types, including focal point electric fires and background heaters, most of which are available in portable and fixed versions. The focal point heater replaces the open coal fire and either stands in the grate or is built into a fireplace unit. Most models are radiant heaters fitted with fuel effect devices to imitate a coal or log solid fuel fire.

Storage heaters first store the heat when switched on and once charged with heat continue to expel it for some hours after they are switched off. A storage heater does not have to be filled with heat before it emits it, but does so when the temperature of the outer casing is raised.

Background heaters, installed to pre-warm a room or to maintain it at a predetermined minimum temperature, are usually of the skirting or panel type or oil-filled radiators. Free-standing convectors are also used for background heating. Fixed heaters are mainly various forms of panel heater, either radiant or convector, and are fixed to the wall at the appropriate height. Infra-red radiant heaters, also fixtures, are especially suitable in bathrooms, where they should be mounted high on the wall out of reach of a person using the bath or shower and in the kitchen and other rooms where space is limited and quick instant heating is required for fairly short periods.

Portable heaters cover almost every type of electric heater except storage. They are used for the main heating of a room or to provide local heating for short periods, and obviously their principal advantage is that they can be carried from room to room as required.

Radiant heaters

The most commonplace type of electric heater used in the home is the radiant electric fire. With loadings ranging from 500 watts to 3000 watts their elements operate at red heat and are usually exposed to touch but protected by a dress guard. Some are reflector fires: *rod elements*, termed pencil elements, are situated in front of a highly polished reflector which directs most of the heat forward into the room. Another form of radiant reflector fire is the infra-red heater, which also has rod elements, but these are thinner and longer than the conventional type, are of lower loading and consist of a wire spiral element enclosed in a silica tube. The conventional rod element is a straight element wire wound on a fireclay former. It operates at a considerably higher temperature than the infra-red rod variety.

Other types of radiant electric fires have bar elements consisting of a brick-shaped fireclay former with a spiral wire element contained in a number of grooves, usually three or five.

Radiant fire elements have various loadings ranging from about 500 watts up to 1000 watts. Heaters in excess of 1000 watts have two or more elements. Loadings of infra-red rod elements are usually under 1000 watts each, and the lengths range from 20 in. to 24 in. (500–600 mm). Loadings of the conventional rod elements are usually 1000 watts, and the lengths are about 11 in. (275 mm). Shorter rod elements of lower loadings are fitted to some models. Fire bar elements are mainly of 1000 watts each.

Another radiant reflector heater is the bowl fire, which has a parabolic polished reflector and a tubular or globe shaped element consisting of a fireclay former with a spiral groove containing the spiral wire element.

Multi-element radiant heaters have built-in switches to provide variation in heat output: one element is usually connected direct to the flexible cord of a portable fire. A 1-bar fire has no integral switch; a 2-bar fire has an integral switch for the second element; a 3-bar fire has two integral switches, one for the second element and one for the third. The exception is a fuel effect fire. The fuel effect indicates when the heater is switched on, and all elements are operated by individual built-in switches. Fixed radiant fires (panel fires) have switches for all elements.

Convector heaters

The convector is box shaped and contains an element unit operating at 'black' heat. With its comparatively low surface temperature this unit heats the air around it, which then rises and flows out through a grille into the room. This air is replaced by colder air which is drawn in through the base of the cabinet, thus creating a continuous flow. The flow continues until the incoming air reaches the cutting out temperature of the integral thermostat. Some convectors have no thermostat and have to be controlled manually; alternatively a room thermostat can be wired into the circuit. Loadings vary from 500 watts to 3000 watts and the cabinet contains a pilot light which produces a warm glow.

Fan heaters

The fan heater is a convector which drives air over elements instead of relying on natural convection. This method enables a greater heat output from a smaller casing because the fan keeps the elements at a fairly low temperature. The fan has a separate switch and can be operated without the heaters and is used as such in hot weather. The heater, however, cannot be switched on without the fan, because the elements would become too hot and damage the unit. The heat output can be varied by means of switches, giving a maximum loading of 3000 watts (some models have lower wattage elements). The unit contains a pilot light, usually a neon indicator.

Combined radiator-convectors

Commonly called 'radiant convectors', these contain radiant elements operating at red heat and a cabinet convector containing a heater unit operating at 'black' heat. The units can be operated together or independently, each being separately switched.

Fuel effect fires

The traditional fuel effect fire is a radiant heater (convectors as well now) with the addition of an imitation coal or log unit, formerly of treated wire gauze but now of plastics. The fuel effect is illuminated by one or more coloured lamps (bulbs), over which are mounted spinners which simulate flames and smoke when driven by warm convected currents of air produced by the lamp.

Some modern versions are motor driven and produce a variety of dramatic effects. The fuel effect can be operated independently of the heating elements so it can be used on a warm evening or on a dull warm day. It also functions as a pilot light and indicates when the circuit switch is on and the flexible cord is 'live'.

Tubular heaters

Available in lengths from 2 ft to 17 ft (0.600–5.100 m), tubular heaters are made of steel or light alloy, are 2 in. in diameter and contain a spiral element supported on mica discs fitted to a spine running throughout the length of the tube. The standard loading is 60 watts per foot run and the tubes operate at a surface temperature of about 180°F. Higher loadings are available and these operate at a higher surface temperature.

The tubes are usually fixed at or near skirting level by means of brackets or they can stand on the floor or be fixed to it. They produce a wide distribution of heat and are especially suitable for background heating. They can be operated as single tubes or can be built up into banks of two or more tiers by adding brackets and fitting a connecting bar.The heat from a single tube is mainly radiant, but as more tubes are added to form a bank the air flow is increased and more heat is produced by convection with a corresponding reduction in radiant heat. A tubular heater installation can be controlled automatically by a

Consumer unit with fuses (*Wylex*)

Consumer unit with miniature circuit breakers and residual current circuit breaker (*MK Electric*)

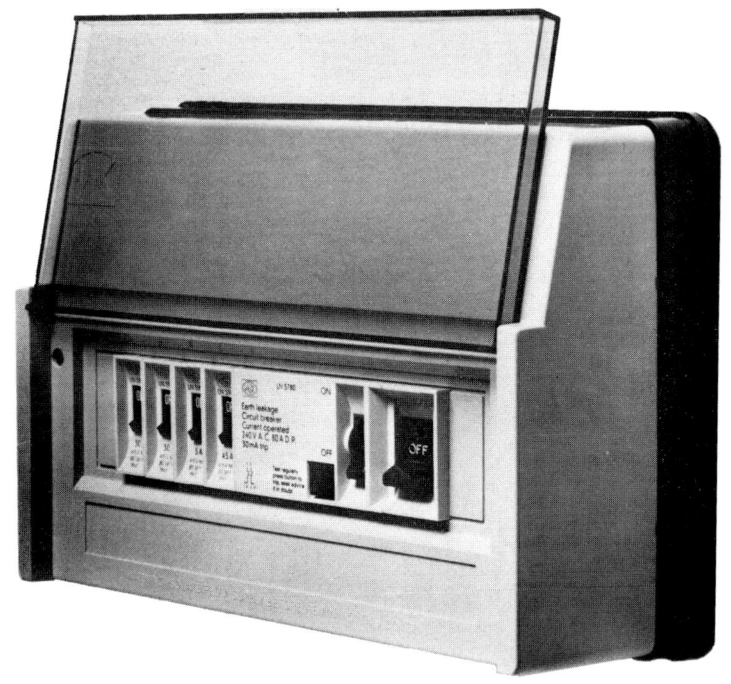

Left: rewirable fuse (*MEM*)

Right: cartridge fuse (*MEM*)

Left: miniature circuit breaker (*MEM*)

Right: residual current circuit breaker (*Allen West*)

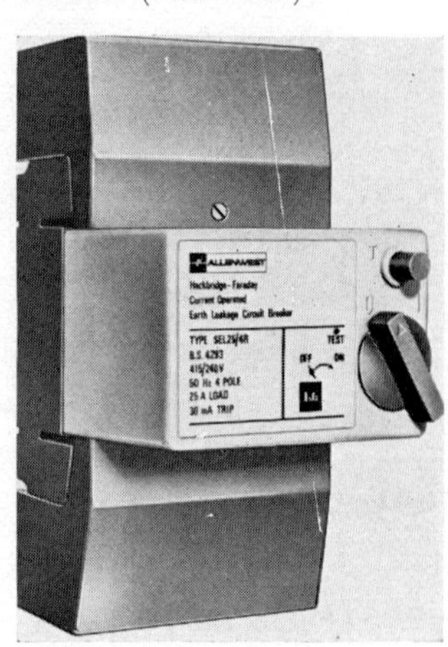

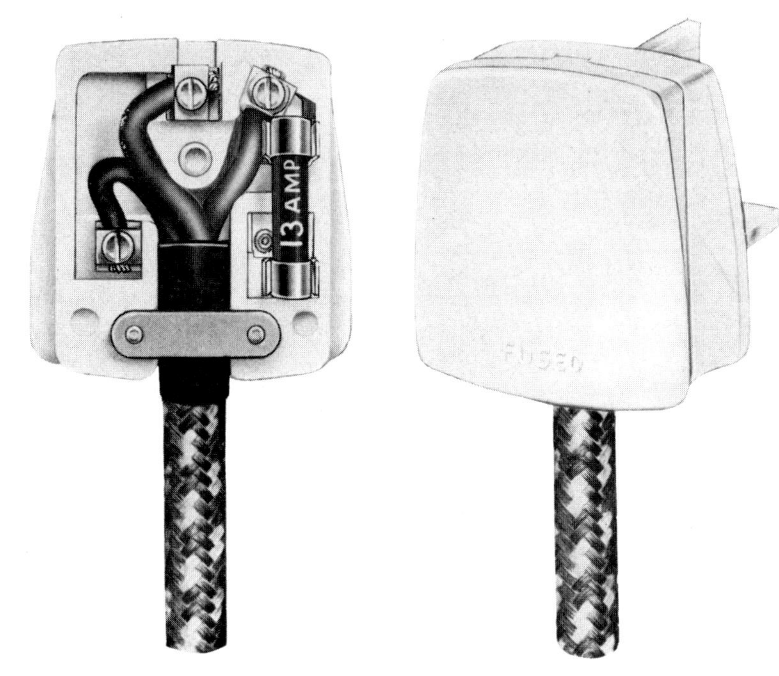

3A fused plug (*Crabtree*)

eft: modern ceiling rose showing terminals and connections (*Rock*)
ight: encased ceiling rose

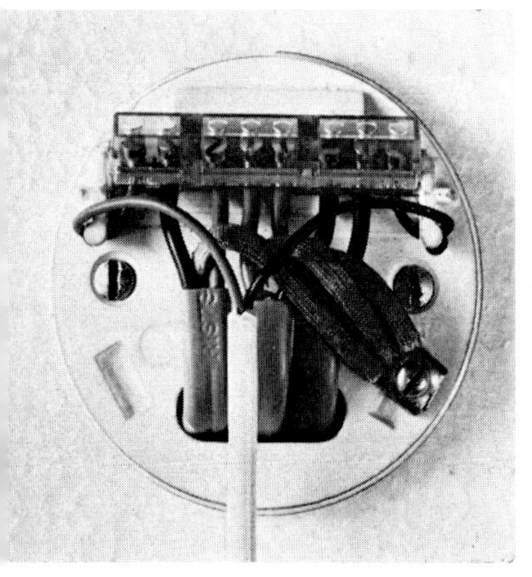

Left: shaver supply unit (*H.H. Electrical*)

Right: fitting immersion heater into flange of hot water cylinder

Dual immersion heater (*Backer*)

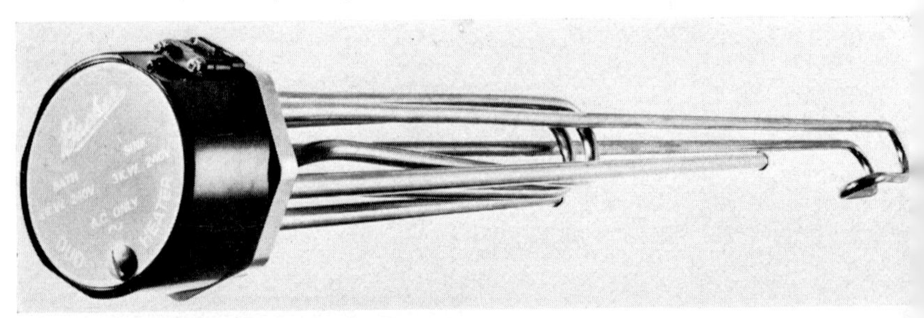

Side entry immersion heater

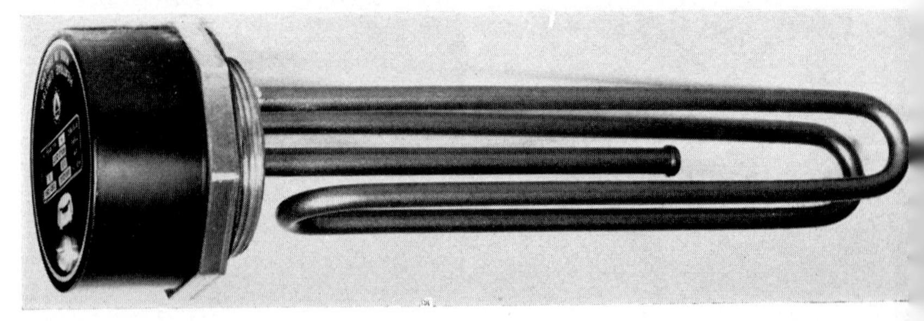

room thermostat, and where desired can also be timed controlled. Special heaters of this type are also made for use in the greenhouse. The electricity supply to a tube or bank of tubes can be from a fused connection unit or from a 13A fused plug and socket-outlet on the ring circuit.

A disadvantage of tubular heaters is their low loading. For example to obtain a load of 2000 watts about 34 ft of tube is required at the standard loading of 60 watts per ft. Using tubes in banks, however, largely offsets this. Their chief merits are flexibility, wide heat distribution and a comparatively low outlay.

Oil-filled radiators

Similar in shape and style to the conventional hot water radiator, the oil-filled electric radiator has a thermostatically controlled immersion element and is excellent as a background heater placed under a window or in any other convenient position.

It is extremely safe in operation, has no exposed elements and can therefore be fixed in a bathroom. Versions are available with a towel rail fitted which on some models is detachable.

Wall panel heaters

Wall panel heaters are made in various sizes, styles and loadings. They operate at a low surface temperature and can be touched without risk of scorching. Suitable for most rooms and in particular the hall, landing and bathroom, they are an alternative to oil-filled electric radiators. The elements are totally enclosed, are usually embedded in the panel and are therefore extremely safe. They can be connected to a fused socket outlet by flexible cord except in the bathroom, where socket-outlets are banned.

7

Electric Storage Heating (Electric Central Heating)

An electric storage heater is basically a block or blocks of thermal storage refractory material containing electric elements, and enclosed in a metal casing with thermal insulation between the refractory and the casing.

They are designed to operate in conjunction with the 'Economy 7' or 'White Meter' electricity tariff or on other off-peak tariffs and are switched into circuit during an overnight period of seven hours. The switch-on period starts about midnight and ends at about 7 a.m., during which time the refractory block is 'charged' with heat. Actual switching times vary in different areas, but in all cases are during an overnight period, when cheaper electricity becomes available.

The stored heat is emitted during the 17-hour day period though heat is also emitted during the charging period. When fully charged at switch-off time heat output is at its maximum, but tends to taper off throughout the day.

There are two principal types: the electric storage radiator, most commonly used; and the storage fan heater, which contains a fan to expel warm air out through a grille.

Electric storage radiators are made in a range of sizes (electrical loadings) starting at 1.7 kW up to a maximum 3.5kW. Storage fan heaters start at 3kW and cover a range of loadings up to about 6kW.

Storage radiators

The heat from a storage radiator is emitted from the metal casing, which is maintained at a fairly even temperature for much of the day. This is controlled by the casing's thermal insulation, which ensures that heat is not radiated too rapidly.

Unlike that of a direct-acting electric heater, the kW loading does not represent the rate of heat output though it bears some relation to it. Loadings vary with the size (bulk or storage capacity) of the heater: the higher the electrical loading the greater the heat storage capacity. Since a storage heater has only about seven hours to accept heat, the rate of charge has to be greater for the higher capacity storage blocks. This means a higher electrical loading.

As a storage heater of higher electrical loading usually contains more heat (when fully charged) but has the same daytime period as all others to expel it, naturally it follows that the rate of heat output must be higher. You therefore choose your storage heaters according to the kW loading, provided they are of the same type when comparing loadings, and you accept that the loading is not the rate of heat output. For example a 3.375kW storage radiator can usually be expected to emit heat at a continuous rate of 1000 watts for much of the day. The length of this period varies, is stated by the makers and is usually for the first 10–12 hours of the day starting at the switch-off time of 7 a.m.

Storage electric radiators are essentially continuous heaters compared with direct-acting heaters, which are switched on and off as required. As such they keep the walls at a higher temperature than that outside and generally provide overall comfort in common with other central heating systems.

The heat output cannot be adjusted by the householder, but there is an input controller to vary the amount of heat stored overnight which, to some extent, influences the output rate next day. For much of the winter the input controller is at a maximum, but in mild weather a lower setting can be satisfactory. To reduce costs, individual heaters can be switched off in rooms not in immediate use, but it is necessary to remember that a heater switched off overnight will not supply heat the following day. Some models have an adjustable damper to provide a boost of heat in the early evening, when the rate of heat output has tapered off from its daytime maximum. Either manually or automatically controlled, this damper usually contains a device which prevents the householder from opening it too early in the day and losing most of the stored heat.

Storage fan heaters

These have more thermal insulation than the storage radiator and as a result their casing temperature is much lower and the output of radiated heat significantly smaller. Heat output is mainly convected warm air. The householder is therefore able to choose the times when the heater is to expel its stored heat either manually by operating the fan switch on the heater, or automatically by means of room thermostats or time-switches (or both) wired into the fan circuits. Devices are usually incorporated to prevent the householder expelling most of the stored heat early in the day.

Positioning

Storage heaters generally should be situated where they will cope with the coldest spots in rooms. Preferably they should be set near a window, but at right angles to it so that the heat is directed across the cold area, but not under the window where much of the heat is likely to be lost via the glass.

Circuit wiring

Since all storage heaters are switched on at the same time it is necessary that each is supplied from an individual circuit originating at a separate fuseway in the off-peak consumer unit. The circuit should be of 20A current rating so that the largest size radiator likely to be installed can be connected to it. Cable used is 2.5 sq. mm twin-core and earth pvc-sheathed house wiring cable. Each circuit terminates at a 20A double-pole switch with a cord outlet fixed near the storage radiator which is connected to this switch by heat resistant 3-core sheathed flex. The switch can to advantage have a neon indicator but it is not essential. Four storage heaters with their four circuits would be supplied from a 4-way consumer unit, but if the immersion heater is also to be supplied from the time-switch controlled consumer unit, an additional fuseway will be required.

Where there are to be fewer than four storage heaters or

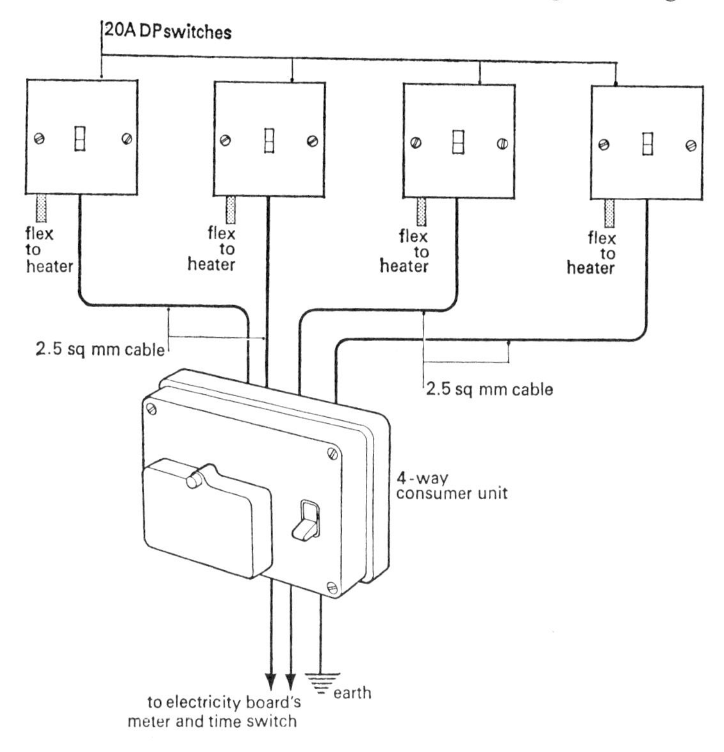

Fig. 11 Circuit wiring for storage radiators

fewer than three plus immersion heaters a 4-way consumer unit should still be fitted, as the 60A switch with this unit is necessary to supply the load. Where no more than two storage radiators are installed and each has a loading not in excess of 3kW, they can alternatively be supplied from a 30A circuit wired in 4 sq. mm cable. Since the fuse rating will be 30A the outlet to each heater must be fused. (These have a current rating of only 13A, which restricts each storage heater to 3 kW.) The consumer unit can be fitted with miniature circuit breakers instead of fuses, and these are preferable.

As already mentioned storage heaters operate during off-peak hours; the necessary time-switch is provided by the Electricity Board, which connects the leads from the consumer unit to it. That is why a separate consumer unit is needed to supply only those circuits which are to be current restricted for the 7-hour night period. All others, including lighting and the ring circuit, are connected to the general purpose consumer unit to receive current continuously. Storage heaters are not connected to or supplied from a ring circuit, because such a circuit is not permitted to supply fixed heaters forming part of a comprehensive space heating installation. A single storage heater having a loading not in excess of 3kW could be connected to a ring circuit provided the householder is prepared to switch it on and off at the beginning and end of the cheap-rate period.

A storage fan heater has to be supplied from two circuits: one supplies the heater and is connected to the restricted-hour consumer unit as for a storage radiator; the other supplies the fan from the unrestricted 24-hour supply so that it can be operated at any time during the day when the heater is not receiving current. This requires a special outlet switch which must be an isolating switch to negate the heater circuit and the fan circuit simultaneously. The one to use is the MK 25A linked switch, which has two flex outlets and is made with and without neon indicators.

As the fan takes only a few watts of electricity, it may be supplied from either the lighting circuit or from the ring circuit via a fused connection unit. A number of fans may be run off the one circuit. Where a room thermostat or a time-switch is used, this is wired into the fan circuit. Each fan can be controlled independently, or one room thermostat and/or time-switch can control a number of heater fans.

Electricaire heating

Electricaire is basically a large storage fan heater centrally situated in the house which provides warm air to all or most rooms via a system of ducting and grilles like other warm-air central heating systems. The unit is available in a number of sizes having loadings of 6–15kW. For the average home a 10.8kW model is a suitable and fairly common loading. The circuit for this size unit has a 45A current rating and the cable terminates in a control unit which contains a heater switch and a switch for the fan which has neon indicators. The unit can be sited in any convenient position.

Although not termed Electricaire units, some of the larger storage fan heaters have facilities for supplying two or more adjacent rooms by means of stub ducting and shutters. The difference between these and Electricaire room heaters is that they supply each room alternately but not usually simultaneously. Selective supply of warm air to individual rooms can also be effected with the Electricaire system by means of adjustable grilles.

Centralec heating

This is the term given to the new wet system of electric central heating. The heater is a modified Electricaire unit containing an air-to-water heat exchanger to supply hot water to a conventional system of pipes and radiators. As the heat is stored overnight during the cheap-rate electricity period, costs compare favourably with the conventional boiler using other fuels.

Floor warming

This heating system uses electric warming cables in the concrete screed of a solid floor normally installed during the building construction. It is especially attractive in blocks of flats, where space is usually at a premium, for this form of heating occupies no space at all. It is a night-storage system but normally requires a midday boost which for new installations is supplied at the higher (day) rate. Costs, though, are comparable with other forms of electric storage heating. Almost any type of floor covering can be laid on the warmed floor, including wall-to-wall carpet. Maximum floor temperature, which occurs at night, is about 80°F (26°C).

Ceiling heating

For domestic use the warming wires are installed before the ceiling is fixed or plastered. The system, although classed as electric central heating, is non-storage and requires a 24-hour supply. The heat emission is by radiation which, near floor level, creates convected currents of warm air that circulate throughout the room.

Thermal insulation

As with any heating system, the house must be well insulated and protected against draughts. It is particularly important to insulate the loft and, where possible, the external walls and to draught-proof external doors and windows. At night, draw all curtains and close doors to reduce heat loss.

8

Electric Water Heating

There are three principal types of electric water heater suitable for installation in the home: instantaneous; storage; and immersion. Instantaneous water heaters supply showers and sinks. Storage water heaters are used for all purposes, especially where large quantities of hot water are required. Immersion heaters are used in conjunction with a solid-fuel system and are fitted into the conventional hot water storage tank. They are also used as the sole means of providing hot water where there is no solid fuel boiler.

Instantaneous water heaters

These have no storage vessel but heat the water as it flows through the unit. Usually they can be connected direct to the cold water mains, the outflow of hot water being controlled by an inlet valve. When the valve is opened the cold mains water under pressure flows into the heater unit, where it is heated and flows out through an open spout or from a shower head. The electric current to the heater element is controlled by an automatic diaphragm switch which is operated by the water pressure: when the water flows the switch is turned on, and it is turned off when the water flow is stopped.

Water temperature varies with the rate of flow: the greater the flow, the lower the temperature and vice versa. It also depends on the electrical loading of the heater elements: the output of hot water from a 6kW instanteous water heater will be almost double that from a 3kW unit.

When an instantaneous water heater is chosen, the loading is therefore very important. Various loadings are: 3kW, 4kW, 5kW, 6kW and 7kW. A 3kW heater is used for hand washing and is fitted over a hand basin; the 4kW and 5kW models are used for supplying the kitchen sink; and the 5kW and 6kW models are used for showers. The 7kW model is intended especially for supplying two outlets in conjunction with a special 2-way faucet valve.

Makes vary in design and styles, of course. Some models consist of a basic unit, in alternative loadings, and can be fitted with hand-washing sprays, showering units and other accessories. Some, such as the Santon 'Imp', are designed simply for hand washing. Another model, made by Sadia, is a press-button unit.

All have an open outlet and must not be plumbed to a closed tap. The pressure of the cold water supply is important: mains pressure is usually adequate, but if supplied from a cold water storage tank at least a 7 ft head of water is necessary.

The electrical circuit too is important. A 3kW model may be run off a 13A fused outlet fed from a ring circuit, but if the outlet is in the bathroom there must not be a plug and socket, but a fused connection unit which, if containing a switch, must be out of reach of a person using the bath or shower. A 4kW unit requires a 20A circuit, and 4kW, 5kW, 6kW and 7kW models require a 30A circuit, and a 30A outlet switch.

Storage water heaters

Basically these are hot water storage vessels containing the water immersion heater to heat it, a thermostat to control the temperature, thermal insulation to prevent undue heat losses, an inlet valve to control the flow and a hot water outlet pipe.

There are three principal types: (i) the *free outlet displacement* type for direct connection to the mains water system; (ii) the *pressure* type, which is supplied from a cold water storage cistern; (iii) the *cistern* type, which is a self-contained unit, complete with its own cold water storage cistern that can usually be connected to the cold water mains supply.

Free outlet storage water heaters

These are single-point water heaters for use at the sink or washbasin, with larger models for the conventional bath. They are similar to the instantaneous water heater except that the water is pre-heated and stored for future use.

Capacities range from 1 gallon to 20 gallons, but unlike the instantaneous type, the heater elements have a maximum loading of 3kW and can be as low as 1kW. The quantity of hot water which can be drawn off at any one time is limited by the storage capacity of the hot water vessel. When this amount has been drawn off it is necessary to wait until more water is heated, and time taken to do this is termed the 'recovery period'. The rate of recovery depends on the electrical loading of the element. When buying a storage water heater choose one which has sufficient capacity for one draw-off with a recovery rate quick enough to meet subsequent demands.

The thermostat setting, which determines the storage temperature of the water, also has a bearing on the amount of hot water available and is usually adjustable from about 90°F (33°C) to 180°F (84°C). For washing dishes you require a water temperature of 140°F (60°C). If the thermostat is set at 140°F (60°C), a 1½-gallon sink water heater will provide 1½ gallons of water at 140°F (60°C) at one draw-off and no more. If, however, the thermostat is set at 160°F (72°C), the 1½ gallons from the water heater mixed with cold water from the tap will provide about 2 gallons of water at 140°F (60°C). Similarly, for hand washing, where you need water at 110°F (44°C), you can get nearly 3 gallons from a 1½-gallon water heater when mixed with cold water.

Although a high storage temperature provides more hot water at usable temperature at one draw-off, there are disadvantages. Heat losses are greater, for these are proportional to the storage temperature. Scaling is also more likely: in very hard water areas the storage temperature should not be higher than 140°F (60°C), but in very soft water areas a storage temperature of up to 180°F (84°C) is permissible, but the heat losses may be excessive. Generally, therefore, the storage temperature—the setting of the thermostat—should not exceed 160°F (72°C) and the size (capacity) of the water heater chosen accordingly.

Storage water heaters suitable for the kitchen sink are available in about six sizes from 1⅓ gallon's to 3 gallon's capacity. They have electrical loadings of 3kW and alternative loadings of 1kW and 3kW. Where a 13A outlet on the ring circuit is available, or a separate 15A circuit can be wired, the 3kW loading should be chosen to obtain the quickest recovery. For normal sink requirements a 1⅓-gallon or 1½-gallon model fitted with a 3kW element is adequate. The recovery from cold of a 1⅓-gallon 3kW water heater is eight minutes, and that of a 1½-gallon model ten minutes. The recovery of a 1⅓-gallon fitted with a 1kW element is twenty-four minutes, and that of a 1½-gallon thirty minutes.

Where larger quantities of hot water are required at the sink a 2–2½-gallon size should be chosen. For the wash-basin a 1⅓-gallon or 1½-gallon model is adequate, but these should have a 3kW loading to ensure good quantities of hot water at peak times. To supply a bath you need a 15-gallon or 20-gallon size. The latter will supply sufficient hot water for two baths in fairly rapid succession, for 12 gallons of hot water at about 160°F (72°C) require about the same quantity of cold to 'fill' the bath with water at 110°F (44°C).

Installing a sink water heater

A displacement—or free—outlet water heater needs very little plumbing. The water heater is fixed to the wall over the sink in a position where its swivel outlet spout will direct the hot water into the sink or washing-up bowl. The cold water inlet of the unit is connected to the mains supply by a short length of ½ in. (13 mm) copper or plastic pipe. The simplest method of doing this is to unscrew the cold water tap, screw in a TEE fitting and refit the tap to the TEE. From the TEE runs a short length of pipe to the inlet of the water heater. For the electrical wiring a length of 1.5 sq. mm 3-core sheathed flex is connected to the 13A fused outlet, which is a switched fused connection unit or a fused plug and socket-outlet. The switch is usually left on and preferably the fused unit has a neon indicator.

Hot water is drawn off by opening the inlet valve. There is a short delay between opening the valve and the hot water flowing, and a corresponding delay when closing the valve and the flow of hot water ceasing. This is because the free outlet water heater has a non-drip device, which prevents water dripping from the spout as it expands when it is heated.

Under no circumstances must the outlet be plumbed to a closed tap. If it were the water, as it is heated, would build up pressure, and should the thermostat 'stick' in the closed position the water heater could explode.

Water-boil sink heaters

Normally a sink electric water heater will not provide boiling water (water at 140°F–180°F (60°C to 84°C) can be used for culinary purposes and brought to the boil in a kettle or cooking vessel), though one make can do so when required. This is the Creda 'Corvette', sometimes termed a wall kettle, which has a non-lagged glass water storage vessel with a capacity just under one gallon. The vessel is graduated in pints on a scale and is filled from the cold water tap by a rubber hose. No plumbing is therefore required and only the quantity of water needed is run into the vessel, which can be anything from two cups up to its full capacity.

The temperature can be adjusted and switched to boiling when required. When the water reaches boiling point an audible warning is given.

This, like most sink water heaters, can be connected by its 3-core flex to a switched fused connection unit, or to a fused plug and socket-outlet. But like any electric water heater when fitted in a bathroom it must, under no circumstances, be supplied from a plug and socket-outlet. A switched fused outlet may normally be fixed in the bathroom for this purpose, but if the switch should be within reach of someone using the bath or a shower it must either be cord operated from the ceiling or a wall switch positioned outside the bathroom door.

Pressure-type water heaters

This type of electric storage water heater is similar to the free outlet displacement type but must be supplied from a cold water system and requires a vent pipe. It will supply one or a number of hot water taps.

The water in the hot water storage vessel is constantly under pressure—the pressure being that of the secondary cold water supply which is determined by the height of the ball valve in the cold water storage cistern in relation to the water heater and the taps it supplies. Plumbing for the water heater and draw-off system is similar to that of the conventional domestic hot water system and storage tank heated from a solid-fuel boiler, but in this case there is no boiler or flow and return pipes.

A cold water feed pipe has to be run from the cold water storage cistern, usually in the loft, down to the cold water inlet of the water heater. A hot water draw-off pipe is run from the hot water outlet, usually on top of the water heater, to feed the various hot water taps. From this draw-off system a vent pipe is run to above the cold water feed tank and is directed down into the tank. As the water in the hot water vessel is under pressure, hot water is drawn off in the conventional manner simply by opening or turning on the hot water taps.

These water heaters are made in a wide range of sizes, from about 5 gallons up to about 100 gallons for domestic use and larger for commercial use. The size chosen depends on requirements. For a one-outlet installation a 5-gallon model would be adequate, but it is better to choose one which will supply all or most of the hot water draw-off positions. For the average home a 20-gallon size is usually adequate and will supply the three taps at the sink, bath and wash-basin. A 30-gallon model is also available; most are dual units but some have one element which heats the full contents of the storage vessel.

Especially suitable and designed for the home is the dual type. This has a storage capacity of 20 gallons and it can usually stand on the floor adjacent to the sink and under the draining board. This heater has two element units: one is fitted near the top in the side of the unit and heats about 6 gallons of water the other, also a side-entry type, is fitted near the base of the vessel to heat the full contents. With some models both elements have a 3kW loading and are controlled by a change-over switch so that both elements cannot operate simultaneously. The switch is marked 'SINK' and 'BATH'—the lower element being switched on when the full contents are heated for a bath or othe purposes and the top element being switched on for normal ho water requirements at the sink and wash-basin.

Some models have a 2kW lower element and a 1kW uppe element so that when the heater is switched to 'BATH' botl elements are in circuit with a total loading of 3kW. In eithe case the maximum loading is 3kW, enabling the water heate to be supplied from a 15A circuit. This must be a separat circuit; not a spur from a ring circuit, because it is a continu ously operated water heater and would deprive the ring circui of 3kW, which would then not be available for portable appliances.

When these dual water heaters are operated on the 'Economy 7' or 'White Meter' tariff a modification of the wiring is made so that the full contents are heated overnight at the cheaper rate, but during the day the housewife can switch on the top element should she need additional hot water. An extra external circuit is required for this daytime facility.

Cistern-type water heaters

These are self-contained electric water heater units for supplying hot water to a number of taps when there is no secondary supply of hot water available from a cold water feed tank. They are made in various capacities from 12 gallons to 30 gallons: the 20-gallon unit is necessary if a bath as well as a sink and wash-basin are supplied. It can usually be fitted on the wall above the bath. Remember to situate it above the highest draw-off tap, because the supply of hot water is motivated by gravity. The wall must be strong enough to support the weight of the stored water as well as the weight of the water heater unit. Some models are floor mounted.

The unit consists of a thermal-insulated hot water storage vessel containing an immersion heater, a cold water feed cistern with a ball valve and a self-contained venting system. The whole unit is inside a sheet steel case. Plumbing involves running a cold water feed pipe (normally direct from the mains) to the feed tank; taking an overflow pipe to the outside of the building; and running the hot water draw-off piping to all the taps. It should be fitted near an outside wall for the overflow pipe, which may be on either side of the unit—the mains feed pipe is connected to the other side.

When choosing the position, sufficient headroom must be allowed for access to the ball valve (the immersion heater is bottom entry, whereas the floor mounted type has side entry immersion heaters). Where there is no other suitable position for a cistern-type water heater it may be fixed in the roof space or attic: this is sometimes necessary in a bungalow to provide an adequate head of water.

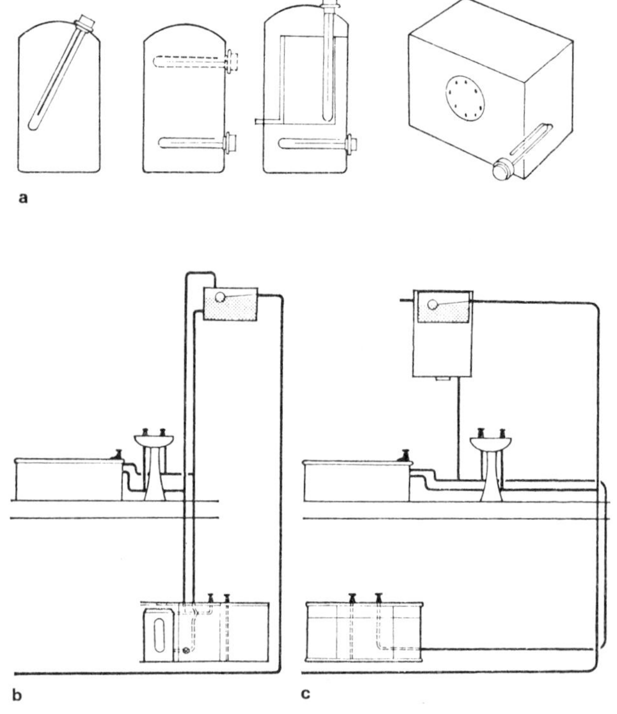

Fig. 12 Water heater arrangements (a) alternating immersion heater arrangements (b) 20 gallon under-sink electric water heater (c) cistern-type electric water heater

Electrical loadings of these heaters are not more than 3kW, enabling one to be supplied from a 15A outlet.

Immersion heaters

An electric immersion heater is a convenient way of providing hot water from the conventional storage cylinder or tank, operated either in conjunction with a solid-fuel boiler or as the sole means of water heating. They are made in a wide range of types, lengths and electrical loadings.

In its most simple form, an immersion heater consists of a mineral-insulated metal sheathed element similar to that of an electric kettle but different in shape. Element lengths range from about 11 in. to 36 in. A thermostat is usually fitted in the heater head, but it is optional and most are of the rod or stem type, adjustable over a range of temperatures from about 90°F to 180°F (33–84°C). The non-stem type have fixed temperatures set during manufacture. The adjustable thermostat should be set at about 140°F (60°C) in hard water districts, and may be up to about 180°F (84°C) where water is soft and scaling unlikely. To reduce heat losses to a reasonable level even when the tank is well lagged the storage temperature and therefore the setting of the thermostat should not be higher than 160°F (72°C).

Immersion heaters are screwed into a flange fitted in the wall of the tank. This flange, and the immersion heater head, has a BSPT thread (British Standard Pipe Thread) of 2¼ in., which is the diameter of the bore of the pipe and not of the flange. This should be borne in mind when the hole in the tank wall is cut.

Either the top of the tank or the side wall are good positions for it. Top entry is normal for the copper cylinder and side entry for the rectangular tank and where there is not enough headroom for inserting or withdrawing a top entry immersion heater.

With top entry it is important that the element extends to within a few inches of the base of the cylinder so that the whole of the hot water is heated. Allowance must be made if the base is concave. A side entry immersion heater must be fitted as near to the base as possible for this reason, and also because water below it will not heat.

To heat and to maintain the temperature of the whole tankful of water can be wasteful when only small quantities are run off during the day, because heat losses are roughly proportional to the quantity of water stored at a given temperature. Known as *standing losses*, these are highest when no water is being drawn off, for then the temperature remains at the maximum set by the thermostat. To reduce this a twin element or dual top entry immersion heater can be fitted which has two elements, one long enough to reach to the bottom of the cylinder and one shorter to heat just a small quantity of water at the top. The short element is usually about 12 in. (300 mm) while the longer element is 32–36 in. (800–900 mm), depending on the size or capacity of the cylinder.

Loadings range from 1kW to 3kW, and the latter is for a

single-element immersion heater. Each element of a twin- or dual-element immersion heater can be 3kW provided they are controlled by a change-over switch to prevent them both from being switched into circuit together.

Twin- or dual-element?

The difference between these two immersion heaters is that the twin-element has one thermostat to control both elements, whereas the dual-element version has two separately controlled elements on the one heater head.

For most applications a twin-element unit is suitable, but where each has to be supplied from a separate circuit the dual version is necessary. An example is where the supply is on the Economy 7 tariff, when the longer element must be on a time-controlled off-peak circuit and the short element on the unrestricted circuit.

Installing an immersion heater

Equipment required for fitting a top entry immersion heater into a conventional copper hot water storage cylinder not already fitted with a 2¼ in. BSPT boss or flange is: one Essex-type single hole 2¼ in. BSPT (57.2 mm) flange, the immersion heater, a tank cutter or hole saw and a 2¼ in. (57.2 mm) BSPT ring spanner. If the cylinder is of the direct type, containing no heat exchanger, the job is quite straightforward.

First cut off the mains water supply and drain the tank; this requires a tap in the system below the level of the tank's base. Using the tank cutter make the necessary hole in the top of the tank on the dome, about midway between the draw-off pipe and the rim of the dome.

Insert a cane or rod into the cylinder to check there is no obstruction. Screw in the flange according to the makers' instructions, ensuring that you do not let the inner section fall into the bottom of the tank, and that you fit the flange washers to prevent a leak. Check the length of the long element by means of the rod. Tighten the flange, using a ring spanner or a wrench. Screw in the immersion heater and tighten in the same way.

Close the drain tap and turn on the water to remove air locks if present. Run off some water to check that the system is operating and that the tank is full. Check for weeping (slight leakage) at the flange, and if there is any it will be necessary to unscrew the immersion heater and introduce some Boss's White or similar jointing compound into the joint. Tighten the immersion heater again and the weeping should have ceased.

If the cylinder is of the indirect type it will be necessary to ensure that the immersion heater will not be fouled by the heat exchanger or calorifier. (An indirect type is recognised by the outlet and inlets which it has in addition to flow and return pipe connections.) The immersion heater must pass perpendicularly into the cylinder and special flanges are available for this. First drill the hole for the flange and check it with a rod. If an immersion heater cannot then be inserted, fix the Essex flange and fit a plug to seal the hole. Some tanks are sold already fitted with the plugged flange.

To fit an immersion heater into a rectangular tank is relatively easy, for these tanks have removable hand hole covers. Before removing the cover buy a replacement gasket. To remove the cover release all the stud screws and clean the old jointing compound from the surface of the tank. Check inside for rusting and remove any sludge. Having decided on the best position for the immersion heaters (ensure no pipes will protrude), fit the flange or flanges, then the heaters, and replace the cover.

When an immersion heater is fitted into an indirect tank or cylinder it is necessary to have a valve in the central heating, or secondary system, to prevent the hot water from circulating through it and so causing unnecessary heat losses and wasting electricity. When the installation is finally complete fit a lagging jacket on to the tank so that heat losses are reduced to a minimum.

Immersion heater circuit wiring and controls

An immersion heater, irrespective of its type, must be controlled by an isolating double-pole switch fitted within reach of a person attending to the heater or thermostat. This is usually a double-pole 20A switch marked 'WATER HEATER', and it can have a neon indicator. The wiring is a 15A circuit from a 15/20A fuseway in the consumer unit. Special controls are required for a dual-immersion heater, and when supplied from two circuits a linked switch is needed. Another variant is a remote control in the kitchen to switch the heater to 'BATH'. The Hotpoint Twimerser has this facility. Alternatively, the change-over switch can be on the heater head itself and hand switched as necessary. Remote control is also possible with two separate main switches: one containing an isolating device at the water heater, this being the master switch, and the other in the kitchen. Both have neon indicators which go on and off together as the switches are operated.

For the Economy 7 tariff there are special controls, some of which enable the housewife to over-ride the time control. One, the 'Backer', is a kit containing two immersion heaters. If a bath is wanted during the day there is a 'One-shot' control which enables the whole tankful of water to be heated, after which it switches off and reverts the system to automatic timed control.

Off-peak storage electric water heaters

These are special jumbo-size water storage heaters designed for the householder to take full advantage of off-peak cheaper electricity. They can be adapted to the Economy 7 requirements and provide an adequate supply of hot water to the household.

Home improvement grants

When you have no bathroom and no room which can be converted into one you can install a shower cabinet fitted with an instantaneous water heater or a shower storage water heater, which can be in the hall, landing, kitchen, bedroom or elsewhere. As this will be the only 'bathroom' in the house it will probably qualify for a government home improvement grant. You should make enquiries about a grant before buying the cabinet and water heater.

9

Wiring Systems

Most domestic circuits are wired in flat twin-core and earth pvc cable of various conductor sizes according to the current rating of the circuit. Some sections are wired in flat 3-core and earth sheathed cable, these being principally 2-way and intermediate switching circuits where one or more lights are controlled from hree or more switch positions. A flat twin and earth sheathed cable comprises two insulated conductors, and one non-insulated conductor. One of the insulated conductors has black pvc insulation; the other has red, with the non-insulated conductor situated between them throughout the length of the cable.

The red conductor is used for the phase wire and the black is used as the neutral. In a lighting circuit the black conductor is also used as the phase conductor where it is the return wire from the switch, this being termed the *switch wire* of the circuit. To distinguish it from the black neutral wire, the ends of a black insulated conductor when used as a switch wire have to be enclosed in a length of red sleeving. This is, however, not always done, so it is necessary to check the wires when replacing switches and lighting fittings.

The non-insulated conductor of a sheathed cable is the protective (earth) conductor of the circuit. Where this is bared of its sheathing at switches, light fittings, socket outlets and joint boxes the ends are enclosed in green/yellow pvc sleeving, which provides the necessary insulation.

Three-core and earth flat pvc sheathed cable used in house wiring consists of three pvc insulated conductors and one which is non-insulated. One conductor is coloured red, another is yellow and the third is blue. The non-insulated conductor is situated between the yellow and blue conductors throughout the length of the cable. The colours represent the different phases of a three-phase electricity supply system, but have no significance when used in ordinary house wiring circuits. However, when the cable is used to link 2-way switches of 2-

way switching circuits, and the three or more switches of an intermediate switching circuit, the colours can be used to distinguish the various wires and connections at the switches. (The bared end of the earth conductor is enclosed in green/yellow pvc sleeving at each switch.)

Although house wiring cables usually have copper conductors, two other materials have been used in the past: aluminium and copper coated aluminium. Aluminium is not now allowed because it sometimes corrodes at joint and terminal connections and hence does not comply with regulations. Copper coated aluminium was used as an alternative to all-copper but is not now manufactured.

Cable sizes

Until 1971, conductors of house wiring cables were made in imperial sizes, which have now been superseded by metric sizes. Where the cables in existing houses are of the old imperial size, all additional wiring must now be with the equivalent metric size cables. The three metric sizes most commonly used for house wiring have single-strand conductors, whereas only the smallest size imperial cable was like this. The next two imperial sizes had 3-strand conductors and the remainder had 7 strands each. When extending existing circuits, therefore, it is often necessary to join new single-strand conductors to the 3-strand and 7-strand type. This does not usually create any problem, but it is something you should know. The various sizes of metric cables, with the nearest equivalent imperial sizes, are given in Table 4. Very large cables sometimes used to connect an installation to the Electricity Board's meter have 19-strand conductors, but only in rare cases will this apply to a metric cable installation.

Cables used for circuits

Sizes used in the home installation are: 1 sq. mm (formerly 1/.044) for 5A lighting circuits; 1.5 sq. mm (formerly 3/.029), an alternative for lighting circuits and also used for 15A circuits supplying a single 13A socket-outlet or connection unit

Table 4 *Pvc-sheathed Circuit Cables*

Cable size *mm²*	*Typical Circuit*	*Fuse or MCB* A	*Maximum length of circuit* metres	 yds
1	Lighting	5	45†	49†
1.5	Lighting	5	70†	76†
2.5	Immersion heater	15	23	25
2.5	Ring circuit	30	80†	87†
2.5	Radial circuit	20	35†	38†
4	Radial circuit	30*	30†	33†
6	Cooker up to 14kW	30	20	22
10	Cooker over 14kW	45**	31	34
25	Meter tails for 100A service			

* NOT rewireable fuse.
** No socket in cooker control unit. If a socket is required, an RCCB must be fitted.
† These lengths assume that lighting points or sockets are distributed evenly along the circuit.

2.5 sq. mm (formerly 7/.029) for ring circuits, for 20A radial socket outlet circuits and for 20A circuits which supply storage heaters and other apparatus; 4 sq. mm (formerly 7/.036) for 30A radial socket outlet circuits, for instantaneous electric water heaters and other single-outlet circuits of this current rating. For a cooker circuit either 6 sq. mm or 10 sq. mm is used, which replace 7/.044 and 7/.052 imperial size cables.

Lighting circuits

A lighting circuit using flat twin and earth pvc sheathed cable can be wired in two ways or a mixture of both. One method is the loop-in system, which is the more popular. The other is the joint box system, which is used for surface wiring and where loop-in wiring is not practicable—for example, for wiring to wall lights which have no ceiling roses or loop-in facilities.

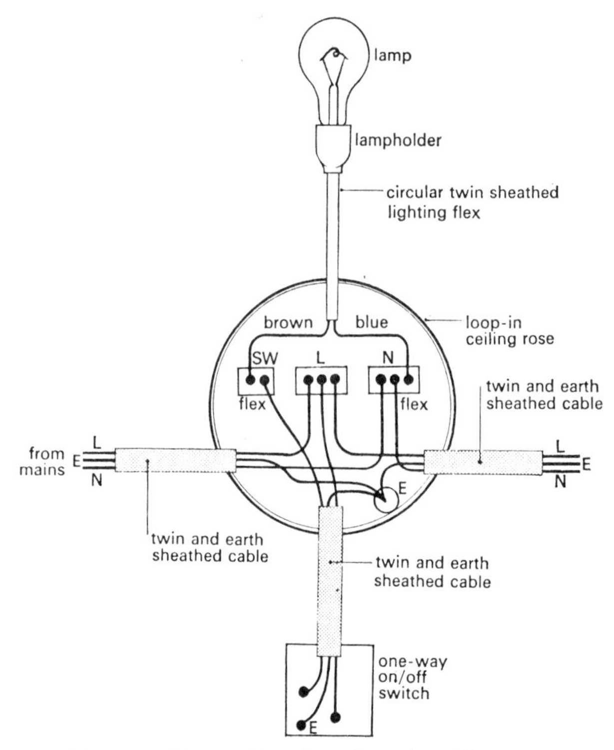

Fig. 13 Connections for a loop-in ceiling rose

The loop-in system

With this system (Fig. 14) a flat twin and earth pvc sheathed cable runs from a 5A fuse or MCB in the consumer unit or distribution board to the phase and neutral terminals of the first ceiling rose in the circuit. From this ceiling rose the cable loops out to the next, then the next, and so on until all the ceiling roses or lighting points have been linked together. A length of the same cable runs from each loop-in ceiling rose to the switch controlling the light.

The joint box system

The same type of cable is used, starting at a 5A fuse or MCB in the consumer unit or distribution board. It runs to a series of joint boxes instead of direct to the ceiling roses or lighting point. It is usually necessary to have one joint box for each light

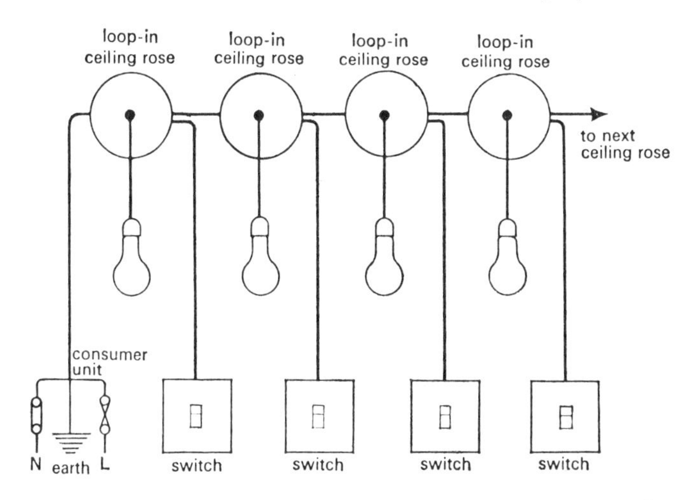

Fig. 14 Wiring a lighting circuit: loop-in system

and its switch (Fig. 15). From each joint box run two similar cables; one to the switch and the other to the lighting point.

Circular in shape, each joint box has four terminals: the phase (live) 'L'; the neutral 'N'; the switch return wire 'SW'; and the earth 'E'. Connections are made as in Fig. 15a. When more than one light is controlled by the same switch (such as wall lights), one joint box is used for all the lights but a separate cable is run from it to each light.

Two-way switching

This controls one light from two different switch positions, for example: a light on the staircase can have one switch on the landing and another in the hall; a bedroom light can be controlled by one switch on the wall near the door and another at the bedhead, usually a cord operated ceiling switch.

There are a number of ways of wiring this. The usual and best method for a sheathed cable system is to wire the light as for a 1-way switch, using a twin-core and earth cable, and to link the two switches by a 3-core and earth cable (Fig. 17a). Both switches are 2-way.

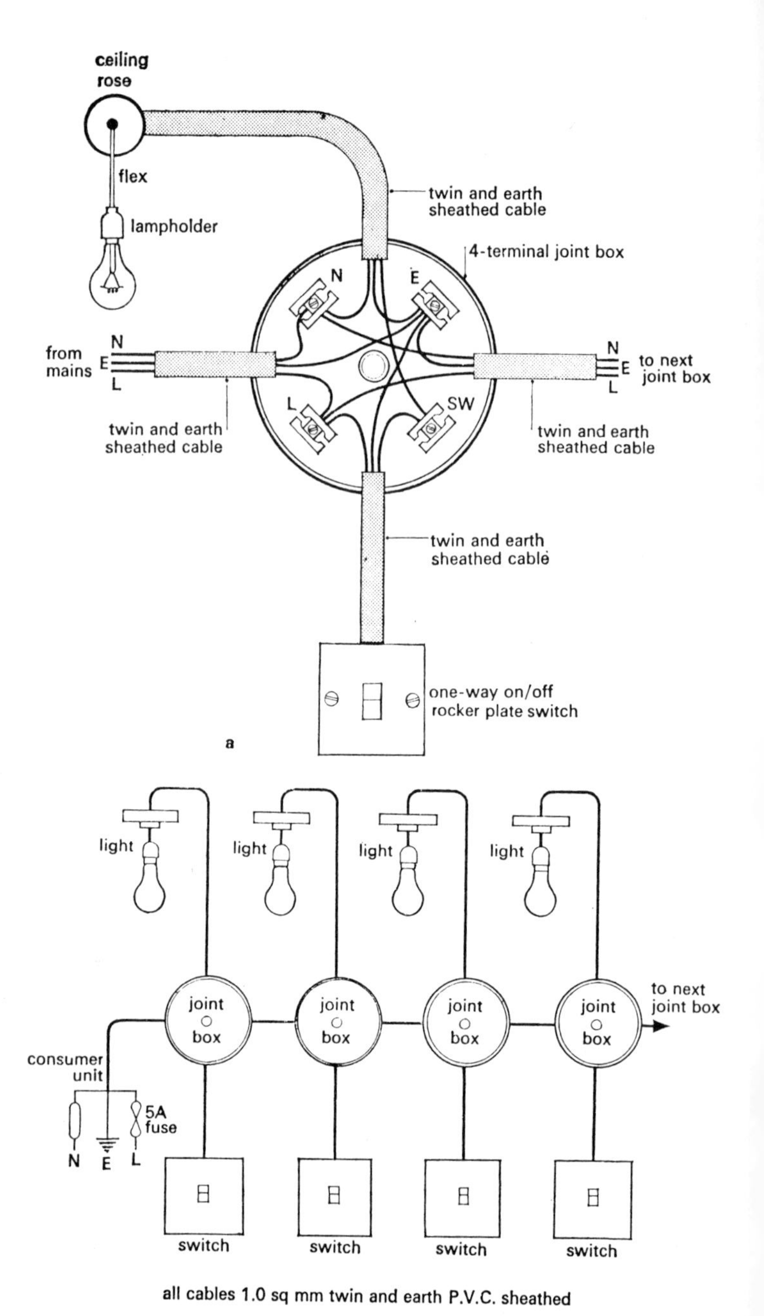

Fig. 15 Wiring a lighting circuit: joint box system (a) joint box connections (b) general circuit layout

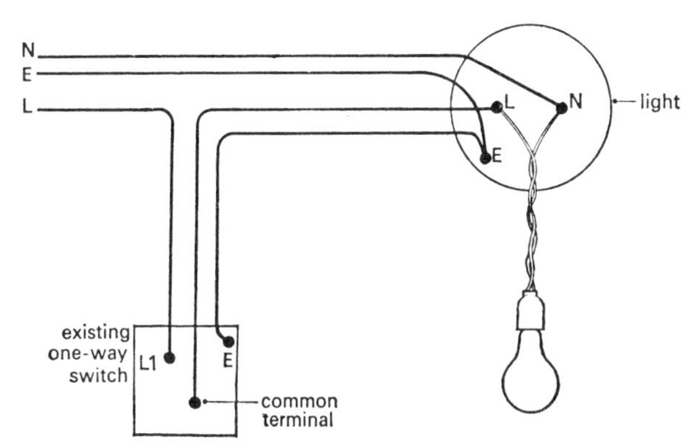

Fig. 16 Switching circuits for lighting (a) one-way switch connections

This method can also be used to convert an existing 1-way switch to a 2-way circuit. The 1-way switch is replaced by a 2-way, a length of 3-core and earth pvc sheathed cable is run from the switch to the second switch position and the connections are made (Fig. 17a).

The conventional 2-way switching circuit is shown in Fig. 17b. With this method a live conductor is run to the 'common' terminal of one of the 2-way switches, a switch return wire runs from the 'common' terminal of the other 2-way switch to the light, and the two are linked by a twin-core (and earth) cable termed the *strapping wires*. This is used in conduit systems but rarely in sheathed cable systems.

Intermediate switching circuits

This circuit enables a light to be switched on and off from three or more different positions. Basically it is a 2-way switching circuit using two 2-way switches, one at each end of the circuit, and an intermediate switch, one for each additional switch position required. These are outwardly identical to 1- and 2-way switches but have four terminals. There are two types each having different internal connections. The circuits giving the external connections are shown in Figs. 18a & b.

Cord-operated ceiling switches are also used for 2-way and intermediate switching circuits. There is no intermediate ceiling

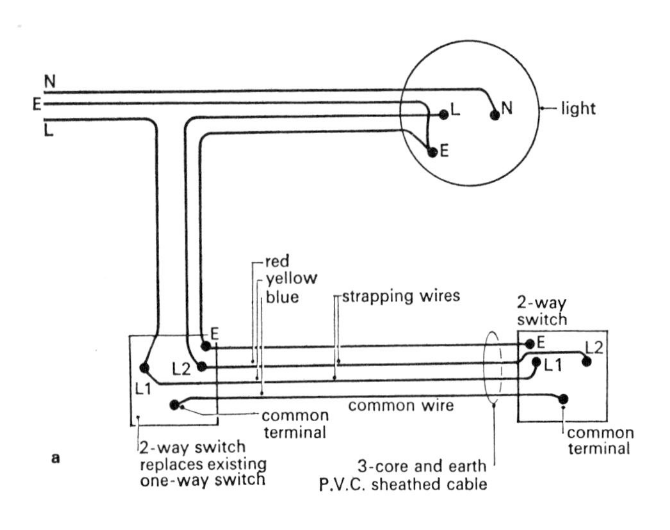

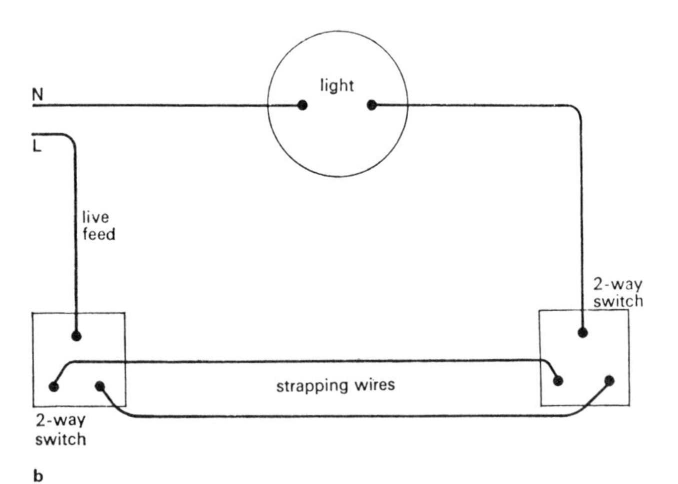

Fig. 17 Switching circuits for lighting (a) 2-way switch connections (b) conventional 2-way switch circuit

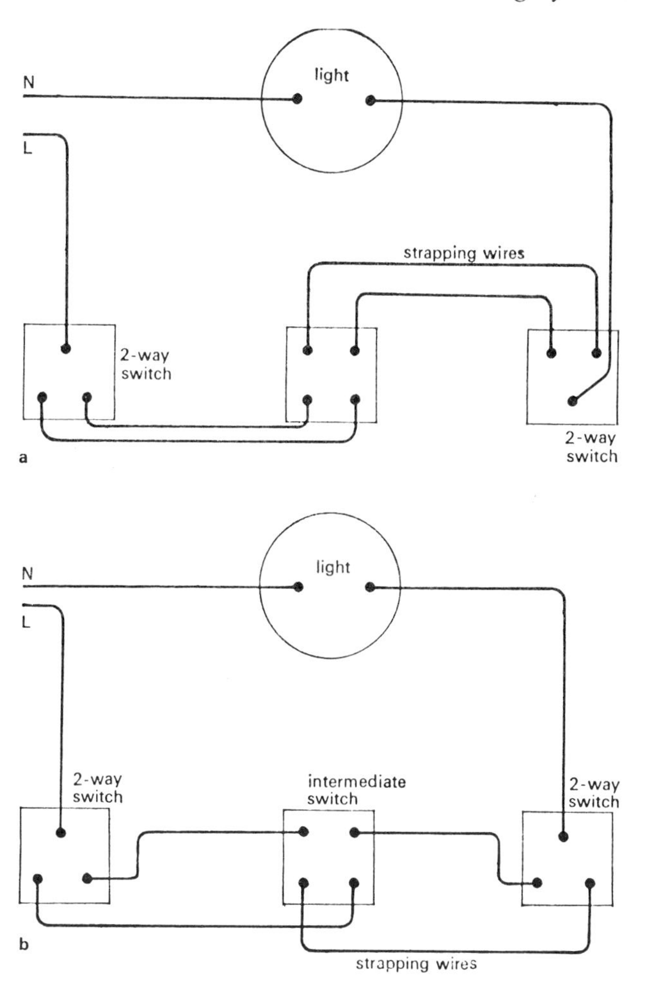

Fig. 18 Switching circuits for lighting (a) intermediate switch connections (b) alternative connections

switch so the ceiling switch must be one or other of the 2-way switch positions of an intermediate switching circuit.

Dimmer switch control

Any light fitting which uses tungsten filament lamps can be controlled by a dimmer switch. These are electronic devices which include a component termed a *thyristor*—a type of transistor—and a printed circuit. No special circuit wiring is required, and it is fitted in place of an on/off switch to vary the light from full brilliance down to off. The dimmer switch fits the standard pattress box used for mounting plate switches.

When used in a 2-way or in an intermediate switching circuit the dimmer switch is often additional, and the other switches operate the light without affecting the setting of the dimmer. This arrangement can be useful in a bedroom or on the landing. Some makes of dimmer switch will replace the 2-way switch itself.

One version of the dimmer includes an on/off switch which enables the light to be switched to full brilliance temporarily without altering the dimmer setting. This is useful during breaks in the television programme or when attending to a child in bed or a sick member of the family.

It is not possible to dim ordinary fluorescent lighting fittings: special fittings and circuit arrangements would be required which are not usually practicable for houses.

Adding a light

This can be done very simply by running a twin-core and earth pvc sheathed cable from the flex terminals of a ceiling rose to the new light. Both lights are then controlled by the one switch but cannot be switched on and off independently. If independent switching is wanted then it is necessary to locate a source of current—a live feed terminal for the switch and a neutral feed for the light—either in a joint box or a loop-in ceiling rose.

From these terminals, and the earth terminal, a 1 sq. mm twin-core and earth cable is run to a new joint box fixed roughly midway between the new light and switch. From there a length of similar cable is run to the new light, and another length is run down the wall to the switch. Alternatively the feed cable can be run directly to a loop-in ceiling rose so dispensing with a joint box, and from this a cable runs to the switch. (A cord-operated ceiling switch will save running a cable down a wall.)

Adding wall lights

Wall lights can be the main lighting in a room, or they can supplement that from a ceiling pendant. They can be independently controlled by a separate switch and each wall light can be individually controlled by its own integral switch. (Not all wall lights have integral switches; many are unswitched.) Alternatively, switched wall lights can be wired from the existing ceiling light and be turned on and off with it, or individually when only the pendant light is needed. This saves running a new cable down to a wall switch. Whichever method is used the principal job is to run the cables from under the floorboards in the room above down to the wall lights below.

A more simple type to install are the pin-up ones, which are fed by flexible cord from plugs and socket-outlets situated adjacent to or immediately below the fitting. Wall lights may also be supplied from fixed wiring connected to a ring circuit via a fused connection unit.

Replacing a ceiling rose

Old ceiling roses can, to advantage, be replaced by the new loop-in type irrespective of the method of wiring (loop-in or joint box system), but the connections are slightly different.

Ceiling roses with three terminals (3-plate ceiling roses) are used with loop-in systems, and those with two terminals (2-plate ceiling roses) are used with joint box systems. In practice you may find this to be the reverse: in the first case one of the three terminals will be blank; in the second case the necessary live cable connection or joint has been made above the ceiling rose, sometimes in the terminals of a pattress box. The new ceiling rose will rectify any discrepancy for it has three sets of terminals plus an earth terminal (see photographs).

The three sets or rows of terminals are *phase (live)*, usually in the centre, flanked by *neutral* and *switch wire*. The outer two contain terminal connections for the flexible cord conductors and are usually marked 'flex'. The live terminal has no flex connection and is shrouded in accordance with regulations to prevent a person touching it.

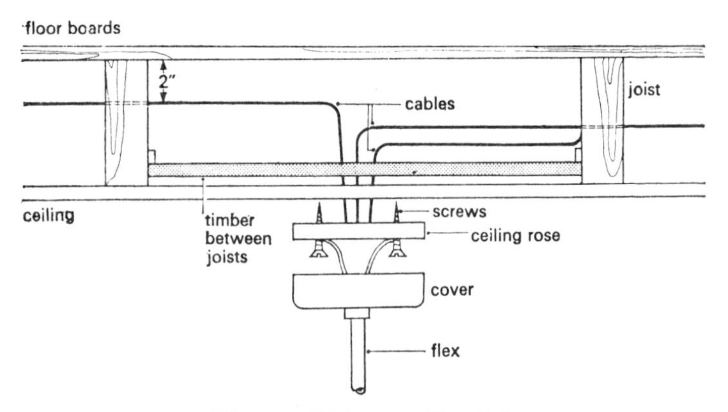

Fig. 19 Fixing a ceiling light

When removing an old ceiling rose first examine the terminal connections, which are exposed on unscrewing the cover. If it is a 3-plate type, only two of the terminals will carry the flex and these must be noted. If the third terminal contains circuit conductors, as it will with a loop-in system, these are the phase conductors and must be connected to the phase (live) terminals of the new ceiling rose. If the third terminal is blank, there is no connection problem for there will only be two sets of conductors to deal with. If the ceiling rose is of the 2-plate type the flex will be connected to both, one core to each, but on removing the ceiling rose check that there are no jointed conductors behind it or behind the mounting block.

Disconnect the cables from the old ceiling rose, taking care not to allow individual conductors to come apart from their joints. To prevent a mix-up, take the phase conductors off first and wrap the ends in a piece of red pvc adhesive tape. The two remaining groups of conductors, or the sole two from a 2-plate ceiling rose, have to be identified before they can be connected to the new rose. One is the neutral and will usually have two or more conductors, which should all have black insulation. The other is usually a single conductor, the switch wire, and should have red insulation or a red sleeve, but this wire is often black too.

If both are single conductors, one red and one black, the black is the neutral and the red the switch wire and should be connected to the new ceiling rose in the normal way. If both are black, as they will be if it is the last lighting point of a circuit wired on the loop-in system, it will be necessary to ascertain which is the live switch wire and which is the neutral. With the mains and the light switch on, test the conductors by touching them with a neon tester (screwdriver): the conductor which causes the neon to glow is the switch wire. As a final check, turn off the light switch and apply the neon tester again to the conductor. This time the neon should not glow. *Don't forget to turn off the mains switch before continuing the job.*

Some old roses, usually plastic types, are fixed direct to the ceiling whereas others, especially when made of porcelain, are mounted on circular wood blocks. If there is a wood block remove it and fix the new rose direct to the ceiling, but take care not to disturb the conductor joints.

Now remove the thin plastic knockout in the centre of the base of the new ceiling rose and thread in the cables, making sure that the sheathing terminates within the rose. Fix the rose with wood screws to a joist or a piece of timber fixed between two joints. (Use a piece of timber 3 × ¾ in. thick (75 × 20 mm) and drill a ¾ in. (20 mm) hole to take the cables.) A ceiling rose or a light fitting must not rely on laths of a lath and plaster ceiling for its sole support.

The conductors are then connected to the terminals of the ceiling rose. One conductor is inserted in each terminal hole of the modern ceiling rose, which mean that jointed conductors are now released taking one joint at a time to avoid mixing up the conductors. If the old lighting circuit has no earth conductor the earth terminal remains blank but you must ensure that only all-insulated or double-insulated fittings are connected. The flex and the lampholder are then fixed to the ceiling rose.

Fitting a new wall switch

The old surface mounted tumbler switch on a wood block is now obsolete and has been replaced by the modern plate switch having a rocker, and with some patterns, a dolly. These switches are mounted on moulded plastic surface pattress boxes or metal or plastic boxes which are sunk into the wall flush with the plaster. As the switches are interchangeable you can mount them first on surface boxes and later, when redecorating, fit them to flush boxes.

The surface plate of the switch is usually 3⅛ in. square and is made in one-, two- and three-gang switch versions, each gang comprising an independently operated switch. The one-gang switch has variations too: 1-way; 2-way intermediate: double-pole; and some special types. For most situations a 1-way is used; for 2-way switching a 2-way version is used. All the switches of the two- and three-gang versions are 2-way. Any 2-way switch can be used as a 1-way on/off switch. When a two-gang switch is used as the two switches in the one position, either or both can be used as 1-way switches. For example in the hall, one switch is used as a 1-way switch for the hall light and the other is used as a 2-way switch for the landing light. An intermediate switch is available only as one-gang and must be mounted separately from others.

Switches and moulded surface pattress boxes are made in

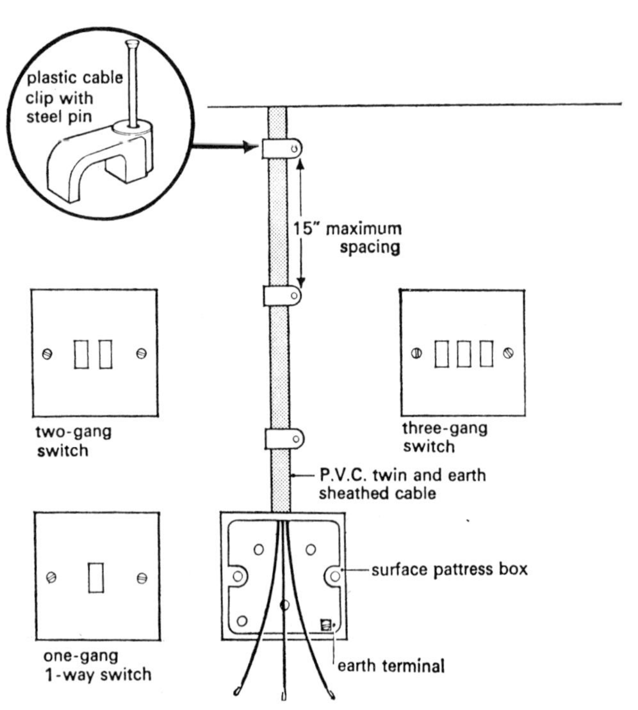

Fig. 20 Fixing a lighting switch to a surface box

various tones of white and ivory and in brown, and their plates differ slightly in style between makes.

Replacing a tumbler switch

Remove the old switch and its wood block from the wall, taking care not to damage the conductors. If the new switch is to be surface mounted, select the surface box and remove the thin plastic to receive the cable. Thread on the cable, making sure the sheath enters the box. Fix the box by wood screws into plugged holes. Connect the ends of the two conductors to the two terminals and secure the switch to the box by the two screws (4BA or M3.5 if metric) provided with the switch.

If, on examination, the insulation at the ends of the conductors is worn they should be enclosed in red pvc sleeving. Or, if the cable down to the switch is run in conduit it may, after checking that there is enough slack about the ceiling, be possible to pull a few inches through and cut off the worn end. Brittle insulation indicates the need for an early rewire.

Fitting a metal flush box is a little more complicated. The flush box for the plates, which is of plaster depth with a rubber or pvc grommet in the top for the sheathed cable entry, has to be pierced to take the cable.

After removing the old tumbler switch and block remove the bits of plaster around the cable and check whether the cable of the switch drop is run in conduit. If it is, the flush box will have to be fixed below the end of the conduit, but first fit a rubber bush on the end of metal conduit if there is not one already. If the switch will be too low in that position you can either fit a surface box, or, if the conduit is plastic you may be able to cut the conduit *in situ*, taking care not to damage the cable. It is possible to shorten steel conduit *in situ* if you can first withdraw the cable. It is a difficult job but usually worth the trouble.

To fit the box: place it in position on the wall and run a pencil around the edge. Chop out the plaster, using an old wide-blade wood chisel or a sharp cold chisel. Place the box in the chase. If it is not flush with the plaster surface, remove sufficient brickwork to give more depth. Thread the cable through the grommet and ensure that the end of the sheath enters the box. Fix the box with wood screws in plugged holes, but before

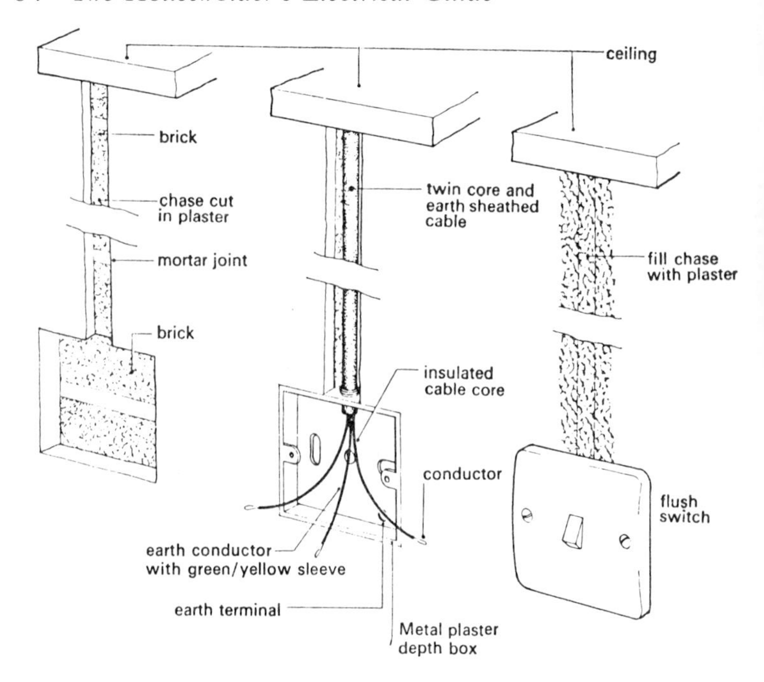

Fig. 21 Fixing a lighting switch to a flush box

tightening them level the box by means of the slotted screw hole. Connect the conductors to the switch terminals and fix the switch with the screws provided.

If the insulation of the conductors is worn or brittle, enclose them in red pvc sleeving as for the surface boxes.

Modern patterns of surface and flush switch boxes have an earth terminal for the circuit protective conductor of the circuit.

Where there is not one, as with most existing lighting circuits, this terminal remains blank until the circuit is rewired with cable containing an earth conductor.

There are also metal plate switches in a variety of finishes. When these are fitted it is necessary to earth each plate by running a conductor to each switch. The cable can be a green/yellow pvc insulated conductor run from the consumer unit. Where the switch drop cable is run in conduit it is usually possible to pass the cable down the conduit alongside the existing cable. Otherwise, the cable has to be run separately or a plastic switch fitted instead.

It is not possible to fit a flush box to a lath and plaster

partition or to a dry partition wall except by chopping out some lath and plaster and inserting a support for the box or by using a special box (in a dry partition wall). You must be prepared for a tricky job.

Running and fixing cables

When installing electric wiring in the house there are a number of details which must be observed to ensure that the work will comply with the IEE Wiring Regulations.

If cables are run under the floor that which crosses floor, joists must be threaded through holes drilled at least 2 in. (50 mm) below the tops and 2 in. (50 mm) above the bottoms of the joists. Alternatively it may be run in slots cut in the tops of joists, but it must be protected from possible damage when floorboards are nailed. If slots already exist, such as when a house is rewired, they can only be used if protected by metal joist inserts made for the purpose. Take care not to weaken the joists by excessive drilling or slotting.

When cables are run through the roof these are not normally threaded through holes in the joists unless the loft is to be boarded or used as storage space. Instead they are fixed to the tops of joists where they are unlikely to be undisturbed. In the vicinity of the trap door and cold water storage tank, which must have access to it, cables are likely to get damaged and are therefore not fixed to the tops of joists.

Cables laid under floorboards at ground level of a house, or under the floor of a bungalow, need be fixed only where they are likely to be disturbed. Normally they are laid on the concrete and require no additional support.

Surface cables

Cables run on the surface of walls and ceilings must be properly fixed using the correct clips. There are various types of clips, but the modern and most simple to use is the pvc clip, which is fixed by a carbon steel pin supplied with each. They range in size for all types of house wiring sheathed cable.

Maximum distances between clips are specified in the regu-

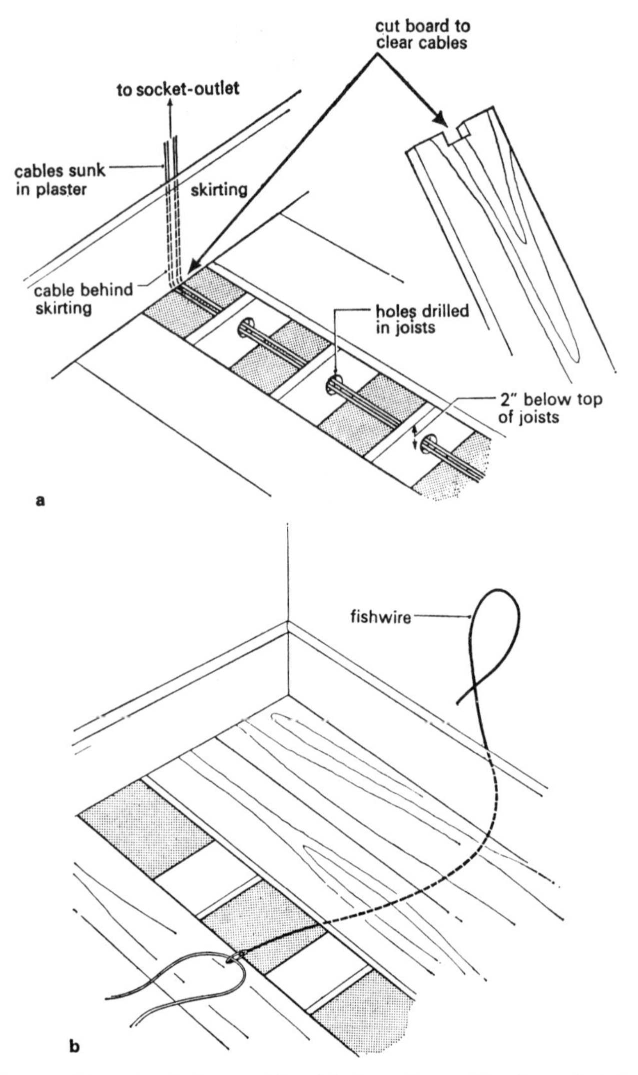

Fig. 22 Running indoor cables (a) threading cable through joists (b) fishing a cable under floorboards

lations. For general house wiring sheathed cables these are: 9 in (225 mm) for horizontal runs and 15 in. (400 mm) for vertica runs. But to eliminate any risk of sagging it is better to reduc the spacings: 6 in. (150 mm) horizontal, 9 in. (225 mm) vertical

Fixing a cable in a straight line is important but not alway easy, and the best way to do it is to first mark a pencil line with a straight edge; or you can use a length of chalked string and 'snap' a line between the two points.

Sinking cables in walls

Because pvc sheathed cables are expected to last the life of the building they may be buried in chases cut in the wall and plastered over without the use of conduit or other additional protection. Also, conduit or casing does not protect a cable from drills or plugging tools. But if you are likely to remove the cable down to switches or wall lights at a future date, it should be enclosed in light gauge oval conduit so that you can withdraw it without disturbing the wall plaster.

Non-sheathed insulated pvc cable must be enclosed in conduit or trunking throughout its length and *must not* be used for ordinary house wiring jobs except in a screwed conduit installation or circuit. The only exception is a green/yellow pvc insulated non-sheathed cable used for earthing purposes.

Conduit installation

Before the last war some houses were wired in light gauge metal conduit complete with metal elbows, tees, and other fittings. These are unreliable for earthing and are usually rewired with pvc sheathed cable and most of the conduit removed or abandoned. At switch drops and similar positions the conduit may be used to carry the new cable but rubber or pvc bushes must be fitted to the ends of such conduit.

Extensions to a conduit installation, such as new lights and other extras, may be run in pvc sheathed cable without conduit and treated as a normal pvc sheathed installation, provided that satisfactory earthing can be achieved.

Trunking

Where floors are solid it is necessary to make alternative arrangements. It is in these situations that cable trunking becomes useful if not essential, be it in a bungalow, a flat or the ground floor of the conventional 2-storey house.

The trunking can be fixed above the skirting board, but it is sometimes possible to replace the wooden skirting by plastic trunking with skirting profile.

In the older house with deep skirtings the narrower modern skirting will not fill the gap left if the old is removed. In this case it is possible to fix the plastic trunking to the existing skirting board. Some trunking incorporates socket-outlets which may be inserted in any position. With other types you can use multi-purpose pattresses made in single- and two-gang versions for single and double socket-outlets and other wiring accessories.

Circuit protective conductors (CPC)

Every circuit of an installation must have a protective conductor, termed the CPC. In sheathed cable wiring the CPC, as already stated, is the non-insulated conductor situated between the two that are insulated. In metal screwed conduit wiring the conduit itself is used as the CPC. In plastic conduit wiring a green/yellow insulated conductor is used for the CPC; and also in plastic trunking, except where sheathed cables containing a CPC are used.

With mineral insulated copper cables (MICC cable) and wire armoured cables used in outdoor wiring, the metal sheath or the wire armour is the CPC.

For most house wiring work the CPC is enclosed in the sheath of the cable. As the ends of the CPC are bare when the sheath of the cable is removed for making the connections at the terminals it is necessary to enclose them in green/yellow pvc sleeving.

Their purpose is to earth the metalwork of fittings and appliances, and connections are provided in ceiling roses and in switch boxes for terminating the protective conductor. Where the switch, like the usual ceiling rose, is insulated and earthing is not needed, the CPC is still at the terminal for use if metal switches are fitted later.

The CPC of power circuits is connected direct to the earth terminal of the socket-outlet, fused connection unit, or cord outlet unit. Some metal boxes used with socket-outlets and other power accessories have an earthing terminal which is used to connect the accessory to earth when the installation is wired in metal conduit, and there is no separate protective conductor. If you buy a box with an earth terminal, this should be linked to the earthing terminal of the socket by a short 'tail' of 1.5 mm^2 green/yellow cable. Do not use this terminal with pvc sheathed cable containing a CPC.

Every circuit should have a CPC running throughout it, but before 1967 one was seldom included in a lighting circuit. A CPC is necessary where metal switches are used or lighting fittings have exposed metalwork. Earthing is particularly important with metal wall lights, for these can be touched by a person who may also be in contact with other earthed metalwork.

Lifting floorboards

When it is necessary to raise floorboards to run the cables underneath you should first look for any which have been raised previously because they will be easier to lift. Tools you need are: a 2½ lb hammer; two electrician's bolster chisels; a cold chisel at least 12 in. (300 mm) long; a nail punch; a tenon saw and a rip saw. A padsaw is also useful.

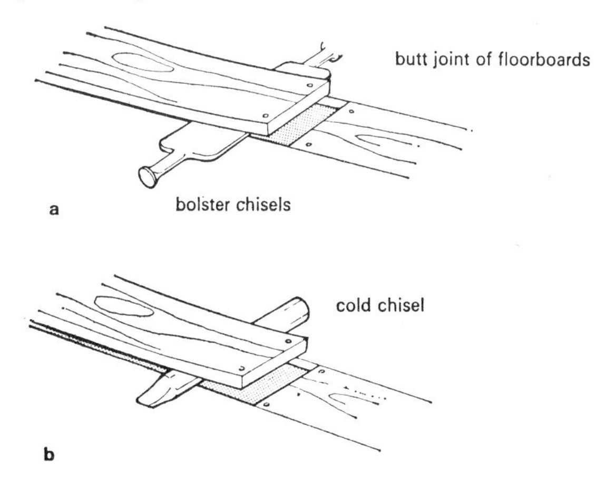

Fig. 23 Lifting floorboards (a) prising floorboard with bolster chisels (b) using cold chisel to hold raised end of floorboard

When a board is lifted for the first time try to select one which is butt-jointed to another and does not extend the full length of the room. Insert a bolster chisel at each edge of the board and lever up the end. Place the cold chisel under the raised end of the board with its ends resting on the adjacent boards. Ease the board up further along its length using the two bolster chisels. Then lift the end of the board and roll the cold chisel along as far as it will go. Release the board and apply a downward pressure on the end. With the cold chisel acting as a fulcrum the remainder of the board will be prised up and with it the fixing nails. This process is repeated until the complete board is lifted and can be wrenched out of the joist under the skirting. Now knock out the nails in the board and extract the others from the joists.

Where a board has no join it will be necessary to cut it at a suitable position. To do this the board must be raised at this point by punching in the nails in three joists, including the joist where the cut is being made. Then, using the two bolster chisels, lift the board at the joist and insert the cold chisel underneath

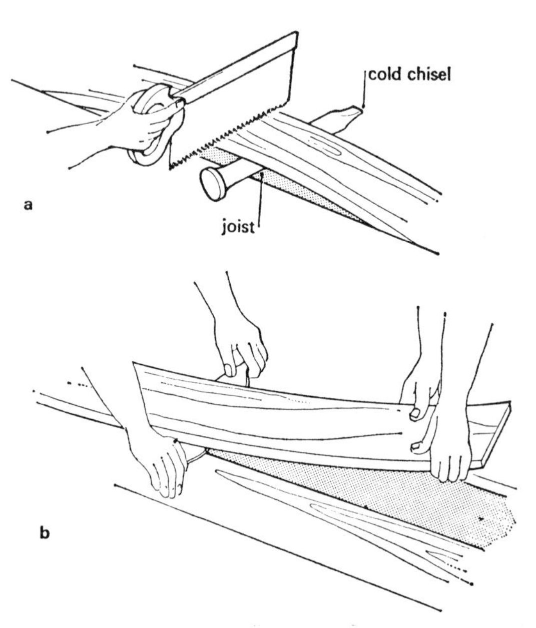

Fig. 24 (a) Cutting a floorboard (b) prising floorboard with cold chisel

near the joist. Using the tenon saw cut the board at a point coinciding with the centre of the joist so that when relaid, both sections of the board will be supported by it. When the board has been cut, the required section or both halves can be lifted in the manner just described.

For T & G (tongued and grooved) boards it is necessary first to cut off the tongue on each side of the board (one being the tongue of the adjacent board). This is done with the rip saw, but it is essential to ensure you are not cutting cables or damaging hot and cold water pipes. When the tongues have been ripped off the lifting procedure is as before.

Replacing boards

When replacing floorboards check there are no bent nails or other obstructions to prevent the board seating properly. Make certain that a board is replaced the right way round and that jointed boards butt each other. Floorboards can be refixed with oval brads (2 in. oval nails), but where covering a joint box and above light fittings, screw them down so that they can readily be raised if necessary. The board above a lighting point need only be a trap extending over two joists. Before fixing these traps insert timber between the joists for securing light fittings.

Boards usually butt against the wall and therefore extend under the skirting board. When a cable passes up the wall from the joist to feed socket-outlets fixed above the skirting this cable, or cables, will foul the board and could be damaged. To prevent this cut a nick in the end of the floorboard as a channel for the cables.

Cables buried in the wall

I have already said that pvc sheathed cables may be buried in the plaster of a wall and so will need no further protection. The ordinary flat twin and 3-core sheathed cable can usually be accommodated in a plaster depth chase, but where the plaster is thin it will be necessary to cut into the brickwork or breeze. The chase can be made good with a plaster filler and papered over or painted. Cables should be chased when redecorating the room. No chasing is necessary in lath and plaster partitions or in interior cavity walls, for the cable can be run down the cavity to a hole drilled in the wall at the outlet or switch position.

When running cables down the cavity of lath and plaster partitions, cross members of timber may obstruct them. Such cross members have to be drilled to take the cable. For drilling a long auger is necessary.

When cables are to be run in conduit down to the switches the oval type of pvc conduit should be used to reduce the amount of chasing required.

Covering cables

Cables run on the surface may be covered in capping made of wood, plastic or metal for a neater job. An alternative method of surface wiring is to run cables in plastic trunking. This is mainly used for wiring ring circuits, using trunking of the skirting type, but it is also used for the lighting circuit wiring, the trunking being of the mini-type including architrave trunking at switch drops.

10

The Ring Circuit

The domestic ring circuit is designed to enable a large number of socket outlets and fused connection units to be connected to one circuit without risk of overloading.

The circuit is protected by a fuse or MCB of 30A and each individual appliance is supplied from it via a 13A outlet. This is usually a fused plug and socket, but for a stationary appliance it may be a fused connection unit, also known as a *fused spur box*.

Any number of 13A socket-outlets and fused spur boxes may be fed from one ring circuit, but the area served by the ring must not be greater than 1080 sq. ft (100 sq. metres). Where the floor area of the house exceeds this, additional ring circuits have to be installed at the rate of one for each 100 sq. metres or part thereof. This restriction limits the likely load on the ring circuit, for obviously, the larger the area supplied the greater the potential load.

If it is known or estimated that the loads connected to a ring serving 100 sq. metres are likely to approach or exceed 30A, the floor area served must be reduced accordingly and additional rings must be installed. This is most likely to occur on circuits feeding modern kitchens or utility rooms for which a separate ring or radial circuit may be necessary.

A stationary electrical appliance is one fixed to the wall, ceiling or floor, such as a wall heater; or built-in or free standing, such as a refrigerator; the load in each case must not exceed 3kW. Electric clocks also come within this category, whether wall-mounted or table clocks, and are supplied from special fused clock connector units. Shaver supply units (shaver sockets) may be connected to the ring circuit too. (There are two types of shaver socket: one has a transformer and is installed in the bathroom; the other kind is much cheaper, has no transformer, and may be installed in any room except the bathroom.) It is regarded as good practice to install two ring circuits in the

2–3 bedroom house even where the floor area is within 100 sq. metres. One supplies the ground floor and the other the first floor. Two circuits should also be installed in the conventional bungalow with the outlets fairly evenly distributed between the two.

Lighting points, although normally supplied from 5A lighting circuits, may within limits be supplied from a fused connection unit connected to a ring circuit.

Wiring the ring circuit

This circuit has a current rating of 30A supplied from a 30A fuseway or miniature circuit breaker of a consumer unit. The cable used is 2.5 sq. mm twin and earth sheathed, wired to form a ring which starts and ends at the terminals of the fuseway.

Socket-outlets or fused connection units for stationary appliances may be connected at any point along the ring. Although this circuit has a current rating of 30A the cable is only rated at about 20A, because each outlet is fed by two cables—the outward and the return.

In addition, others may be fed from spurs branching off the ring cable, to supply outlets in remote positions. The number of spurs which may be connected is restricted to the number of socket-outlets and fixed appliances connected to the ring cable: if there are, say, eight outlets, eight extra spurs may be wired.

Any one spur may supply not more than one single socket-outlet, or one double socket-outlet, or one fixed appliance. A ring circuit with eight socket-outlets on it may have eight spurs each supplying one double socket-outlet making a total of sixteen, plus eight on the ring cable which is a grand total of twenty-four. In practice there will normally be fewer spurs than permitted in the regulations, because it is usually better to connect most sockets directly to the ring, leaving the spur facility for future extension.

Spur cables are the same size and type as used to wire the ring. They may be connected to the ring cable either at 30A 3-terminal ring circuit joint boxes or at the terminals of socket-outlets and fused spur boxes (fused connection units). When looping a spur cable out of a joint box it is best not to cut the ring cable. Instead, remove the required amount of sheath and

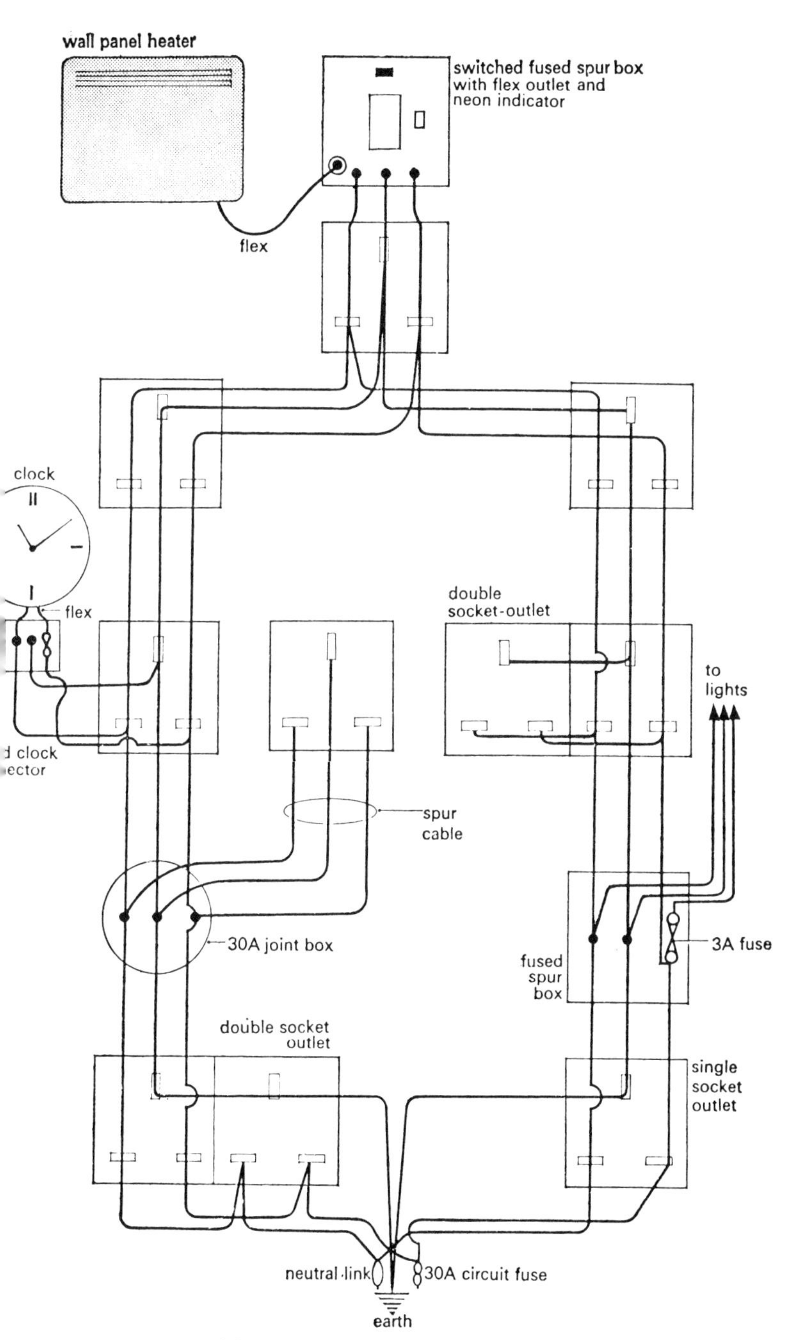

Fig. 25 Typical ring circuit

insulation, lay the bared conductors into the terminals with the ends alongside the ring conductors and tighten the terminals. As the earth conductor is not insulated, do this with green pvc insulation tape.

When adding a spur cable to the terminals of a ring socket-outlet or fused connection unit, place them by the sides of the existing conductors and tighten the terminals. As the 2.5 sq. mm cable is a solid single-strand conductor, it is not possible to twist the ends in the form of a joint. Also, do not attempt to insert more conductors than the capacity of the terminals. Only one spur can be connected to any one joint box or socket-outlet, so do not try to exceed this.

Fused spurs

The ordinary spur, as we have seen, is solidly connected to the ring cable at the joint box or socket-outlet. Others, known as *fused spurs*, may be run from the 'LOAD' or 'OUT' terminals of a fused spur box. These are therefore protected individually by the spur fuse and may supply a number of outlets having a total capacity of 13A or less.

Wall lights can be supplied from a fused spur as can a bathroom heat/light unit or heater where no socket-outlet or switch is permitted if within reach of a person using the bath or shower.

The 13A socket-outlet fitted to domestic ring circuits is made in a variety of types: single-, double-, and three-gang. There are switched and non-switched versions, and switched versions with neon indicators. Most types can be fitted on to metal boxes sunk flush into the wall, or they can be fitted to surface boxes. Some patterns are designed for surface mounting only. All 13A plugs have fuses, but some versions are switched and have a neon indicator (so do some non-switched 13A fused plugs).

Fixed heights

The recommended fixing height of a socket-outlet should be not less than 6 in. (150 mm) above the level of the floor or a working surface such as in the kitchen.

However, it is more convenient for old or disabled people to have sockets situated higher on the wall, say at one metre above the floor level. This saves them having to stoop to withdraw the plug or switch off the socket. Where young children are concerned it is better to keep the sockets nearer the floor to avoid trailing flexes, which can cause accidents.

Radial circuits

Radial circuits are multi-outlet circuits supplying 13 amp outlets and are available in two current ratings: 20A and 30A.

A 20A radial circuit may supply an unlimited number of 13A socket-outlets and fixed electrical appliances from 13A fused connection units, within an area not exceeding 20 m^2. The circuit is wired in 2.5 mm^2 twin and earth pvc flat sheathed cable, originating at a 20A circuit fuse of the rewirable or cartridge type or an MCB (miniature circuit breaker) in the consumer unit.

A 30A radial circuit may also supply an unlimited number of 13A socket-outlets and fixed appliances from 13A fused connection units within an area not exceeding 50 m^2, which is two and a half times the maximum permitted area for a 20A radial circuit. The 30A circuit is wired in 4.0 mm^2 twin and earth pvc flat sheathed cable originating at an MCB or a cartridge-type circuit fuse—*not* a rewirable fuse.

11

Outdoor Wiring

Electricity can be used satisfactorily and with safety outside the house provided the work is carried out correctly using the proper cables and equipment. For most householders outdoor wiring consists of running a cable to a detached garage, workshop, shed or greenhouse. But when electricity is required to power a fountain, a pump in the pool or garden lighting, or to supply an electric mower, hedge trimmer or other electrical garden tools, points usually need to be fixed outside to eliminate trailing flexes from the house. Outside lights attached to the house and the switches which control them also need to be wired properly.

Electricity to outdoor buildings

As a detached building or other outdoor point of utilisation is outside the equipotential zone formed by the main bonding within the house, the circuit supplying it must be protected by a residual current circuit breaker (RCCB) having an operating current of 30mA.

It is usually convenient to connect the outdoor circuit to a spare way in the consumer unit. If the unit is of the modern type incorporating 'DIN rail' mounting for the protective devices, it is possible to fit a combined MCB/RCCB, but otherwise the RCCB should be installed separately adjacent to the consumer unit.

The RCCB or MCB acts as the isolating switch for the circuit, but an additional switch may be provided where the supply enters the detached building to afford local isolation. If this additional switch is omitted, the MCB or RCCB at the origin of the circuit must be capable of being secured in the 'off' position so as to prevent inadvertent reclosure.

Outdoor equipment which is used only occasionally, such as

electric lawnmowers or hedge trimmers, may be plugged into a socket-outlet in the house designated for this purpose. The socket must be labelled 'For equipment outdoors' and the circuit must be protected by a 30mA RCCB; alternatively, the RCCB may be incorporated in the socket outlet.

Wiring to detached buildings

Permanent wiring may be run overhead, underground or along a wall but *not* on a fence, which would afford inadequate support for the cable. The type of cable used depends on the method of installation.

Overhead method

For this you can use ordinary sheathed house wiring cable suspended from, or attached to, a catenary wire strained between the house and outbuilding. If the span between the house and garage or shed is not more than 10 ft (3 m) you may dispense with the catenary provided that the cable is attached to rounded supports so that no undue strain is placed on the conductors or insulation and precautions are taken to prevent chafing. For this distance too the cable may be run in an unjointed length of heavy gauge steel conduit. The minimum height above the general ground level for the cable alone is 12 ft (3.5 m) but where contained in conduit it is 10 ft (3 m).

For longer spans, where supported by a catenary, the cable at its lowest point must not be less than 12ft (3.5 m) above the general ground level or 17 ft (5.2 m) if there is access for vehicles beneath it.

The catenary is fixed by an eye bolt or other suitable fastening at one end, and to a straining eye bolt at the other. For very long runs down the garden an overhead cable needs intermediate supports, usually poles.

The cable is either fixed to the catenary by insulation tape and clips or is suspended from it by special rawhide or plastic slings. The catenary cable should be bonded to earth but must not be used as the circuit protective conductor. This is contained within the cable itself.

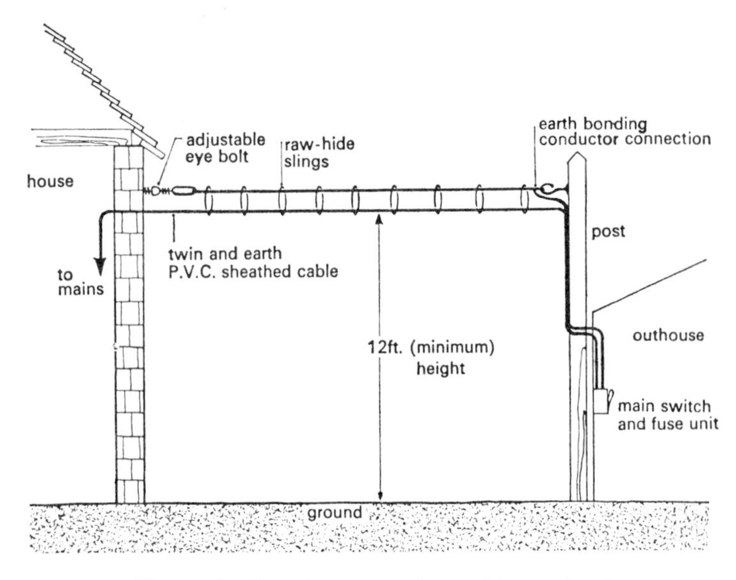

Fig. 26 Running an outdoor cable overhead

Underground method

A cable laid underground between the house and outbuilding must be buried at least 18 in. (500 mm) below the surface of the ground. Preferably route the trench where the ground is unlikely to be disturbed in the future: the edge of a lawn or pathway is usually satisfactory. If the cable has to cross a vegetable plot or other places where deep digging is likely, a trench deeper than 18 in. (500 mm) is advised. The presence of the cable should be indicated by cable covers or marking tape laid immediately above the cable.

Two cables recommended for running underground which may be buried direct in the soil are: (i) armoured cable which has an overall extruded pvc sheath—usually black; and (ii) mineral insulated metal sheathed (MICC) cable which has an overall extruded covering of pvc, usually orange in colour. This covering is to protect the galvanised steel wire armour of the armoured cable, or the copper sheath of the mineral insulated cable, from the corrosive effect of the soil. The cable is twin core of the appropriate size and current rating for the circuit, the wire armour or the copper sheath being used as the circuit protective conductor.

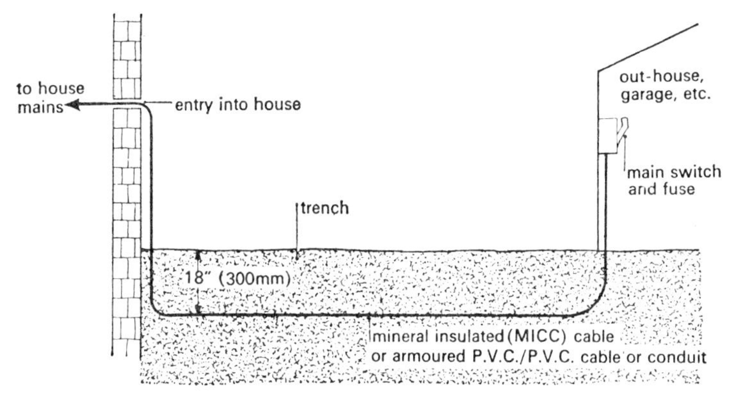

Fig. 27 Running an outdoor cable underground

An alternative underground system is twin-core and earth pvc sheathed cable run in conduit. The conduit must be either heavy gauge galvanised steel, which is preferred, or rigid pvc. Steel conduit must be bonded to earth but must not be used as the circuit protective conductor.

Terminating and jointing underground cable

Mineral insulated cable must have a seal fitted at each end to keep out the moisture because the insulation is hygroscopic. Fitting seals is a fairly difficult job requiring special tools and materials but the cable can be bought in cut lengths already fitted with the seals. When the cable is terminated in a metal junction box or into a screwed outlet of a fitting or wiring accessory it requires a screwed gland. The glands are fitted at the same time as the seals, so it is better to buy the cable with both seals and glands fitted.

Armoured cable also requires a gland at each end to contain the wire armour and to ensure a good electrical connection for the earthing in the junction box or accessory. Where the supply position in the house or the isolating switch in the outbuilding is some distance from the point of entry of the underground cable, it is better to terminate the underground cable in a junction box and run the remainder of it in ordinary twin-core and earth house wiring cable. The junction box to use is the metal knockout type used for mounting socket-outlets flush with the wall. The two ¾ in. (20 mm) blanks are removed from the box sides. These accept the glands of the cable, which are secured by brass screwed bushes or steel conduit locknuts, but first the edges of the holes must be cleaned of enamel to ensure good earth connection and continuity. The boxes are fitted with blanking-off plates which serve as covers.

Where cable is run in conduit for the underground section of the outdoor circuit no junction boxes are needed, as this cable runs direct to the switches in house and outbuilding. The conduit is terminated at the point of entry in the building. If steel conduit is used it is fitted with a rubber bush to protect the cable sheath.

Choosing the right type of cable

Armoured twin and earth cable is the best for underground purposes. It is easy to handle and as pvc insulation is non-hygroscopic no sealing of the ends is required. Also for its current rating it is less subject to voltage drop when loaded to capacity.

The next best choice is mineral insulated copper sheathed cable. This has the advantage of being smaller in diameter in sections where it runs on the surface. It can normally enter the house via an air vent above the damp course, except if bought fitted with seals when it will not pass through a vent hole.

Conduit, the third choice, is more difficult to install. If it is of steel, threads have to be cut for jointing which needs stocks and dies—not normally part of a householder's tool kit. Plastic conduit is fairly easy to install and the cable requires no seals or glands because it is ordinary sheathed.

Surface method

Only where there is a wall extending down the garden, or for most of the run, is this method possible for under *no circumstances may cable be fixed to a fence*. Cable is, however, frequently run on the exterior wall of the house to feed outside lights and switches.

The best cable to use in this situation is mineral insulated copper sheathed, with an extruded pvc covering of orange colour. Armoured cable and also heavy gauge galvanised steel conduit may also be fixed to and run along an outside wall, but both are unsightly. Where appearance is unimportant armoured cable can be used.

Outdoor sections of cable which feed an outside light or switch fixed to a wall of the house or garage may be ordinary twin and earth, provided that it is not liable to mechanical damage. It is often possible to run the cable inside the house or building and pass it through the wall immediately behind the outside light or switch. This may mean altering the chosen positions of the light (or switch), but it is worth it to save the outdoor run.

Cable run along outside walls is secured by clips, fixed at the same maximum distances as for inside runs: 15 in. (400 mm) apart for vertical runs and 9 in. (250 mm) for horizontal runs.

Outdoor cable sizes

Cables supplying an outside garage, workshop, shed or greenhouse must be of adequate size to carry the load and to ensure there is no significant voltage drop on long runs.

A cable which feeds just a light in a shed a few feet from the house need not be more than 1.5 sq. mm run from a 5A fuseway in the house. For most situations where there is likely to be other equipment used, the minimum size is 2.5 sq. mm from a 20A fuseway, this being a 20A radial circuit. For long runs of 50 ft or more and where heating is to be installed you should install a 30A circuit using 4 sq. mm cable. A 30A circuit using 4 sq. mm cable should be run to a heated greenhouse.

Cable running to an outside light or switch fixed to the house or other building needs to be only 1.5 sq. mm in size, but for socket-outlets in the garden 2.5 sq. mm size cable must be used where these are of the 13A fused plug type. Mineral insulated cable is buried in the soil in the same way as running a cable to an outside building. The socket-outlets should be fixed to a garden wall or to stout posts, at a height of not less than 6 in. (150 mm) above ground level. Weatherproof socket-outlets are used, which may be metal clad or unbreakable rubber fitted with hinged covers.

12

Electric Bells, Buzzers and Chimes

The ordinary domestic electric bell usually operates at the low voltage of between 4½V and 8V. It is called the trembler bell because of the trembling action of the electro-magnet and contact system. It operates equally well on DC from a battery and on AC from a mains transformer. Some domestic bells, as with their commercial counterparts, operate on AC only and have a different contact system from that of the trembler bell. If an AC bell is connected to a battery it will only produce a single strike each time the push is operated and the circuit closed.

A buzzer is constructed similarly to a trembler bell, or an AC bell, but has neither striker nor gong. The contacts, which have only a small gap between them, produce a high note which has been compared to the wings of a bee in flight—hence the name.

A bell circuit, also used to supply a buzzer, is very simple and as the bell operates at extra low voltage (elv), below 50 volts, the wire used is only lightly insulated and is known as bell wire. The battery or transformer to supply the circuit can be situated in any convenient position and in some models it is contained in the bell casing itself.

Twin (2-core) bell wire is normally used for the circuit, since it is much neater, when run on the surface, than single wire. One length of twin bell wire is run from the battery or transformer to the bell; another length runs from the bell to its push. As it is twin wire a joint has to be made in one of the conductors at the bell. The wire is fixed with insulated bell staples, or alternatively self-adhesive wire is available.

The bell push, fitted at the front door, is made in a variety of styles and types including illuminated versions which contain a small torch bulb. An illuminated push is possible only when the bell, buzzer or chimes are powered from a mains transformer: the bulb, which is alight continuously, except for the

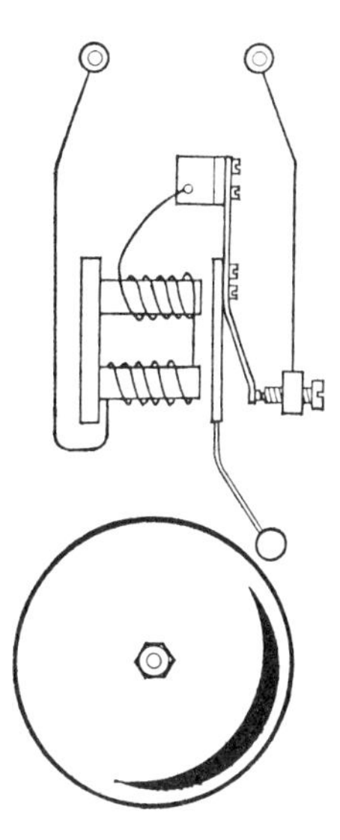

Fig. 28 Interior view of trembler bell showing connections and contacts

moment when the push is being operated, would drain a battery within a day. The bulb, within its push, is connected across the two terminals of the push and is in effect wired in series with the bell. It does, in fact, provide a continuous closed circuit but as the current required to operate the bell, buzzer or chimes is greater than that required to operate the bulb a slight movement in a bell is sometimes noticed, but this is usually insignificant. The light from the bulb goes out when the bell push is pressed because the push contacts short circuit the bulb to let the current flow through the push contacts.

Bell transformers

The mains transformer supplying current to the bell circuit must be of the double-wound type with an earthed secondary winding. An auto-transformer which has a single winding may not be used to supply a bell or other elv appliances. Proprietory bell transformers sold in the shops for the purpose are double-wound and meet the required regulations.

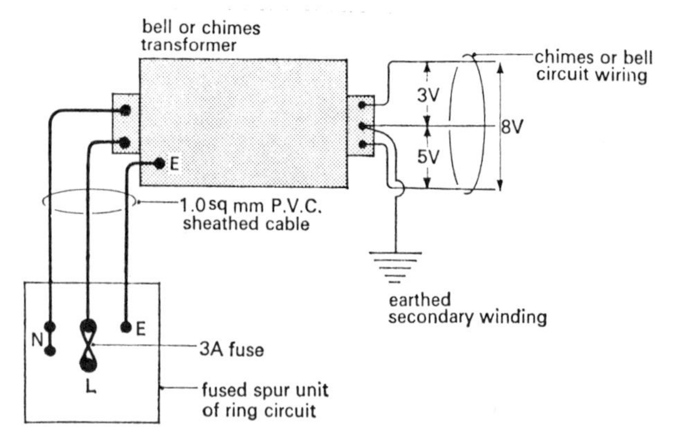

Fig. 29 Mains and bell circuit connections to a transformer

The transformer is supplied from the mains voltage wiring, the circuit and cable of which must be as for any other mains outlet or point. The cable, 1 sq. mm twin-core and earth pvc sheathed, may be looped off a lighting circuit, either at a ceiling rose containing a live terminal as well as the necessary neutral, or it can be connected to a feed cable on the lighting circuit by inserting a joint box. Alternatively the transformer can be supplied from the ring circuit via a 3 amp fused connection unit. The mains cable is connected to the 240V input terminals of the transformer, the phase conductor to one and the neutral conductor to the other. The circuit protective conductor is connected to the earth terminal of the transformer, or if all-insulated with no earth terminal it is connected to the centre terminal on the low voltage side of the transformer.

The three output or secondary terminals of the transformer give a choice of three voltages for the bell circuit. These are usually 3V, 5V and 8V. The ratings are marked but the two outer terminals are always at the highest of the three voltage outputs. The 3V and the 5V tappings are used for bells or buzzers; the 8V tapping is used for door chimes. There are also bell transformers which provide other voltages, the most common being 4V, 8V and 12V. The 12V supply is required for some models of chimes: this is specified by the makers in the instructions supplied.

A bell or a buzzer can be operated from two push positions, such as at the front and back doors, but such an arrangement

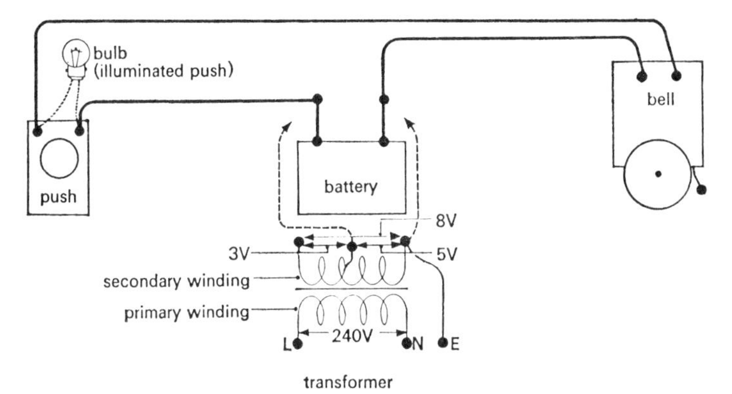

Fig. 30 Bell circuit powered alternatively by battery and transformer

is only satisfactory using two bells with different notes or one bell and one buzzer. Two separate circuits are necessary, one for each, but both can be powered from the one battery or transformer because the likelihood of both pushes being operated simultaneously is remote.

Bell gongs are made in four types, each giving a different tone. These are: round gong, the most commonplace of the four; sheep gong, the next in popularity; church gong, used for special purposes; and wire gong, which is a rare bell which produces an especially pleasing note. A front door single bell arrangement can be utilised to provide a second push station in, say, a bedroom or a sickroom, simply by running a twin bell wire from the push or the bell to the second push. By arranging a code, such as three rings for the sickroom, interpretation of calls is possible.

Extension bells

Where a second bell is required as an extension from the existing single push at the front door there are three ways of arranging it. The two bells can be (i) wired in parallel; (ii) wired in series; (iii) operated in conjunction with a change-over switch so that either bell—not both—will ring according to where you want to hear it.

Parallel connection is not always satisfactory, because there

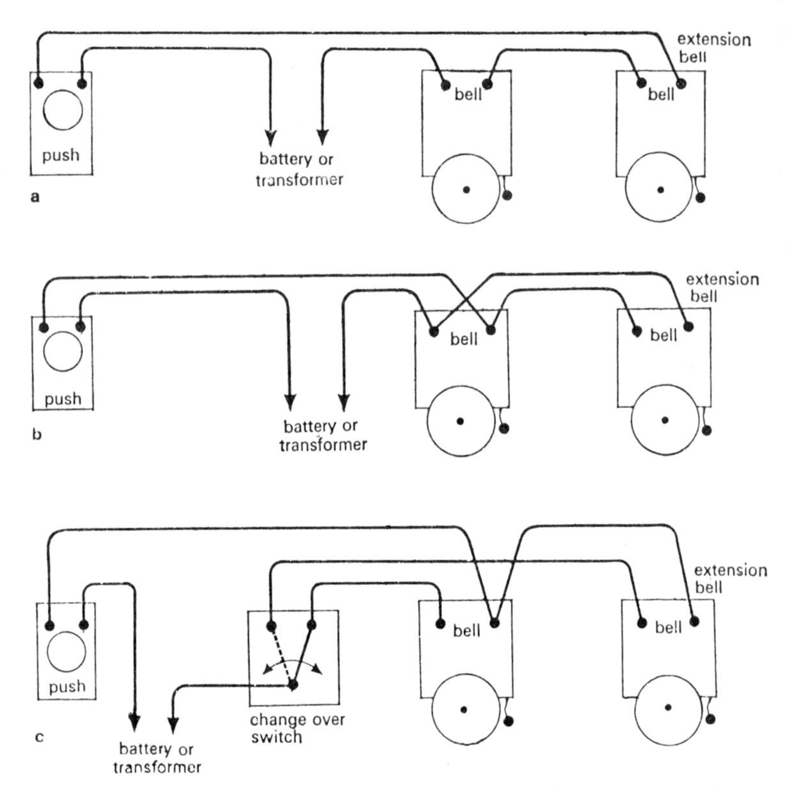

Fig. 31 (a) two bells wired in series (b) two bells wired in parallel (c) two bells controlled by change-over switch

is a tendency for one bell to deplete the current of the other. It is therefore necessary to step up the voltage of the supply, either by adding more cells in series with the existing battery, or by using a higher voltage tapping on the transformer. But that is not the complete solution, for the bells must also have equal impedance: they must match, and for this the wiring to the extension has to be taken into account. It is even more important that the bells are equally tuned by adjusting the contact setting screw. A more satisfactory arrangement can be made by connecting the bells in series, but one must be modified. Two trembler bells, unless they are synchronised and remain so, will only ring intermittently, if at all. When the contacts of both bells are open no current will flow in the circuit. The second bell in the series must either be a single-stroke bell or a trembler with the contacts shorted out so that it acts as a single stroke bell. As the trembler bell operates and alternates the current flow in the circuit, the single stroke bell also operates with a trembler action at the same frequency as the parent bell.

The most reliable arrangement is the change-over switch, which allows only one bell to be operated at any one time. The only disadvantage here is that the switch must be manually operated each time the bell is needed at the extension position, and then switched back to the main bell. A change-over switch can be an ordinary 2-way light switch connected as in Fig. 31c.

Door chimes

Door chimes are made in a variety of types and styles. Some have just a double note which emanates from one push—at the front door. Others provide both a double and a single note—the double note for the front door and the single note for the back door. Some use musical notes or church bell chimes. A few models are battery powered and some only work from a mains transformer. Others can be operated from either. The power source of some models is contained within the chime casing; for others the battery or transformer must be external.

The wiring circuit is the same as for a bell, but the connections on the chimes vary with the model. The makers always supply a connection diagram, so there is no problem.

Faults in bell circuits

When a bell, buzzer or chimes fail to operate, first check whether the battery needs changing, or, if the unit is transformer powered, whether the circuit fuse has blown or the supply has been switched off—if locally switched at the outlet.

The most common fault occurs in the contact system and is usually rectified either by cleaning dirty contacts or by adjusting the contact screw. Two other faults can be that either the cover has fallen off the bell and fouled the striker arm, or that a circuit wire has broken (this is usually at a staple or where the wires are exposed to damage). A sticking plunger is a common fault on door chimes.

If the lamp of an illuminated push does not operate, first check the circuit fuse and then take out and test the bulb. A dirty contact on the bell or a loose connection in the circuit will cause the bulb to go out.

13

Domestic Electrical Appliances

Domestic electrical appliances are generally well designed and well made and can therefore be expected to give good service over many years, but they must be treated with care and be serviced periodically.

Many of the smaller servicing jobs can be undertaken by the householder but to attempt to overhaul the larger appliances, termed in the trade 'white' appliances, is inviting trouble. These, which include refrigerators, freezers, washing machines, spin driers and also storage heaters, should be serviced only by mechanics who have been trained for the job. Replacing a broken or worn component often means dismantling the appliance using special tools and equipment. Even the apparently simple job of replacing a belt on a spin drier or twin-tub machine may involve this, which is beyond the knowledge and capability of the householder. Such servicing also requires a makers' manual which, unlike the motor car manual, is usually only available to authorised dealers and servicing firms.

To ensure that you can expect reasonably good service from your appliances you should buy only those made or distributed by reputable firms who have a good servicing organisation to carry out repairs. Most appliances sold in Britain carry a label which signifies they have been tested and approved electrically safe by the British Electrotechnical Approvals Board. Some appliances come within the BEAB scheme but do not carry labels. This does not mean that all appliances not approved, or that imported appliances are unsafe, because there are a number of good reasons why some are not submitted for approval by the makers.

You should be careful about buying second-hand appliances and preferably buy only from firms you know to be reliable. Do not use an appliance you have picked up cheaply at a jumble sale until it has been properly tested. Don't give damaged or faulty appliances to a jumble sale. Those you send for scrap should be made beyond repair or they may be resold and result in an accident.

Types of appliances

There are three principal types of domestic electrical appliance: (i) those with a heating element, which include fires and cooking appliances; (ii) power-operated appliances such as vacuum cleaners and food mixers; and (iii) power-operated appliances which also have a heating element, such as hair driers and fan heaters.

General repairs

When a portable appliance fails to work, first check the plug fuse. Remove the fuse from the plug and fit a known good one of the same current rating. Test the old one and if blown discard it immediately. If the fuse has not blown, examine the flex for obvious signs of wear or damage. If both fuse and flex are all right it will be necessary to make a more detailed examination as outlined in the following pages. *Before you carry out any inspection or repairs to a portable appliance first remove the plug from its socket-outlet.*

Repairing electric fires

The most common fault in an electric fire is a broken or loose element, or a broken or damaged flex.

Pencil rod elements of reflector fires are secured by: (i) milled nuts; (ii) spring clips; or (iii) dagger type end caps which fit into spring loaded recessed contacts.

Loose contacts resulting in sparking is a common fault with the milled screw type, but this can usually be rectified by tightening the milled nuts. Sparking between the rod terminal screw and the end of the element wire is also common, but easily cured by tightening the terminal screw.

A pencil rod element consists of a fireclay hollow rod with a straight wire element wound in a continuous groove. It is not

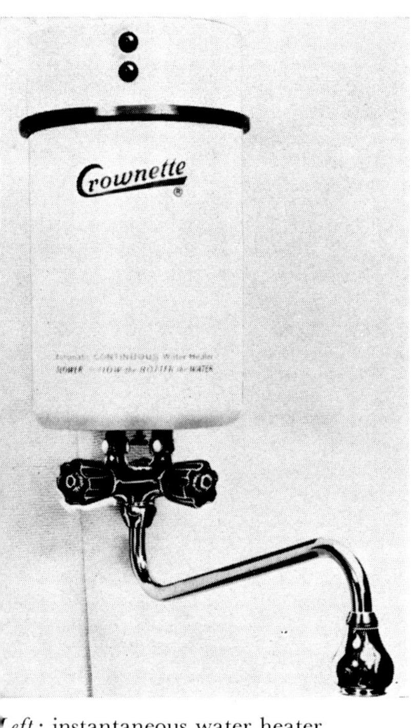

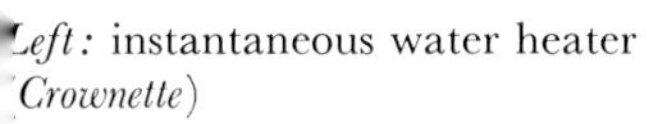
Left: instantaneous water heater (*Crownette*)

Right: storage water heater (*Santon*)

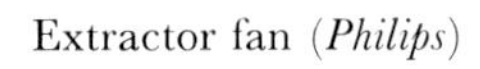
Extractor fan (*Philips*)

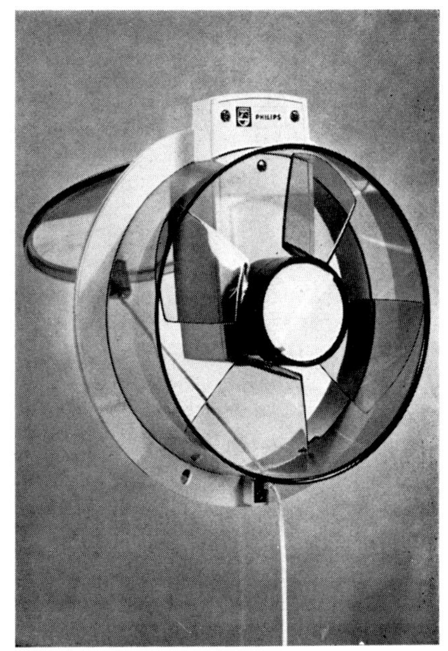

Convector heater (*Carniscot*)

Fuel effect radiant heater (*Sunhouse*)

Left: oil-filled radiator (*Hurseal*)

Right: washing machine, front loader (*Hoover*)

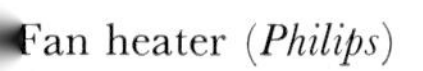

Fan heater (*Philips*)

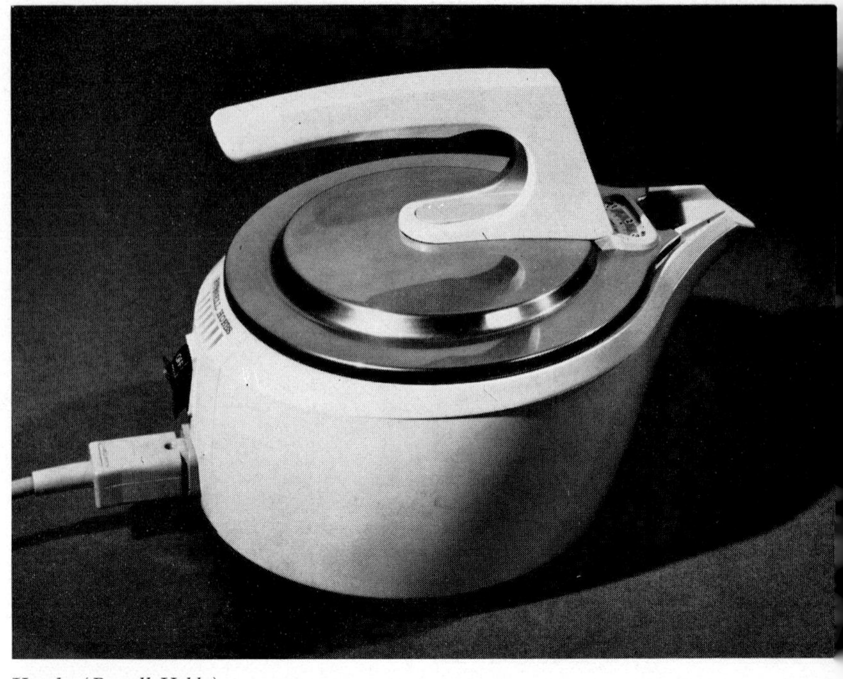

Kettle (*Russell Hobbs*)

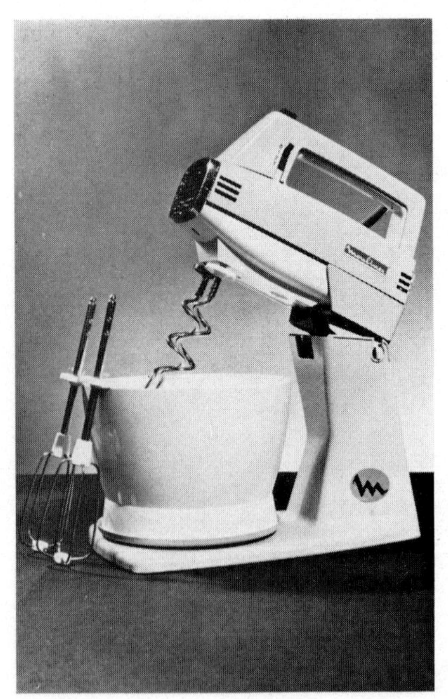

Food mixer (*Moulinex*)

practicable to rewind an element wire, so when it fails the complete rod has to be replaced. A break in the wire is either obvious, or has produced a blob of melted metal, or can be located by running a pencil along the coils. The element can be mains tested on the bench using a pilot lamp, but this has a high fire and shock risk and should be left to the expert.

Pencil elements are made in a range of lengths and loadings

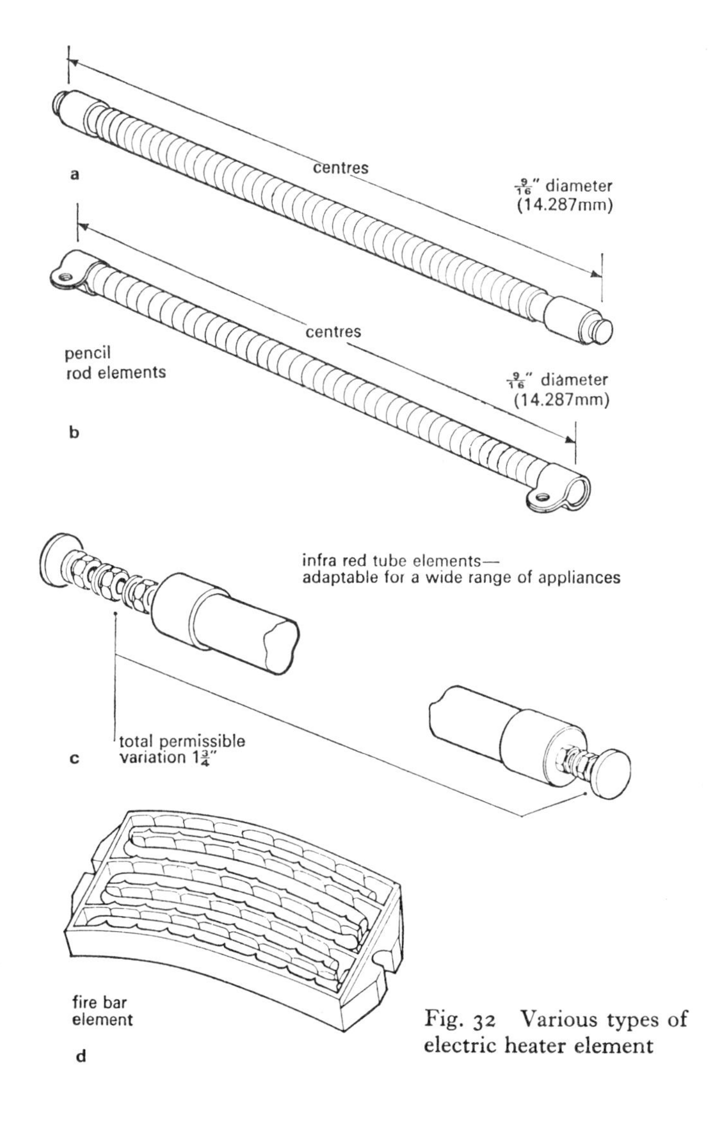

Fig. 32 Various types of electric heater element

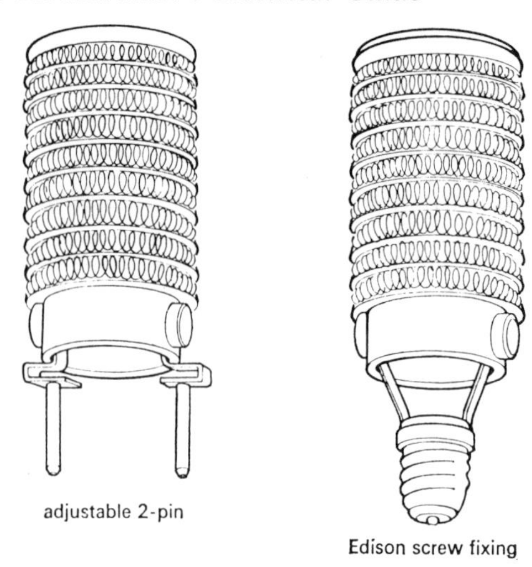

Fig. 33 Two types of bowl fire element

and with a variety of end caps. When replacing an element it is essential for it to be the right length with the correct end caps. Adjustable elements are available, giving a length variation of about 2 inches, but are made in only the milled screw type. To remove a pencil element it is necessary to remove the milled nut or 'spring' the other type out of the clips, having first taken off the dress guard in front of the heater.

A single-element portable electric radiant fire, including reflector types, has no built-in switch: the element is energised when the power plug is inserted or the socket of the switched type is switched on. This is a safety device to indicate when the flex and heater are 'live'. A multi-element fire, without fuel effect, has one non-switched element, but the remainder are usually individually switched. A fuel effect fire usually has all elements individually switch-controlled because the imitation coal or logs or other luminous device serves as the visual indicator.

As the non-switched element in multi-element fires is the one most frequently used, this is the element most likely to fail first. You can delay the failure time by swopping elements occasionally. From the safety angle, it is important for the element of a single-element radiant fire and the non-switched element of a multi-element fire to be replaced as soon as they fail, even if this means 'robbing' one of the others. The lamp of a single-lamp fuel effect fire should be replaced without delay for the same reason.

Infra-red reflector fires

The elements of these fires are also of the rod type but are wire spirals enclosed in silica tubes. If the element has failed, but the tube is intact, you can fit a new spiral to the existing tube, but it is far more satisfactory to buy a new element complete with silica tube and end contact caps.

The elements are made in a variety of lengths and in different loadings and with different types of end caps depending on the make and model of heater. It is therefore essential that you buy the correct replacement.

Fitting a new element

Remove the dress guard; release the screws holding the shields covering the ends of the element. Release the element from its fixture—this varies with the model. Insert the new element, replace the end shields and finally the dress guards.

Wall-type infra-red reflector fires often have built-in cord-operated switches. If the cord breaks you can usually fit a new one to the existing switch, but if the switch fails you will need a new one.

Bowl fires

Bowl fires are reflector fires which have a spiral wire element fixed in grooves of a fireclay former, either cylindrical or spherical in shape. A new spiral can be wound on an existing former provided it is of the right length, and loading.

The complete element is secured to the fire assembly by (i) plugging it in; (ii) screwing it into an Edison screw 'lamp-holder' or (iii) securing it with nuts and washers.

If the fireclay former is fractured the replacement must be identical. To rewind the former, remove the dress guard; release the complete element; carefully unwind the old spiral; measure its length; stretch out the new spiral about 3 in. short of the old one and wind it on, securing and connecting it. Do not stretch it too much or it will sag when wound on the former, causing coils of the spiral to 'short' and burn out the element. Replace the element and the dress guard.

Fire-bar radiant fires

The elements of this type of radiant fire are wire spirals fixed in grooves of a flat fireclay element (also known as brick-type elements). Those such as the Belling, Fig (32d.) have five grooves. If the fireclay bar is intact you can fit a new spiral to the bar. The old spiral is removed by releasing the clips and disconnecting the ends of the terminals. Divide the new spiral into as many sections as there are grooves, one coil of the spiral at each end of each section being straightened to go round the ends of the grooves. The old fixing clips can usually be used again.

To remove a fire-bar element from the heater it is first necessary to take off the back panel by releasing nuts or screws; then you can disconnect the wires. These are usually stiff and uninsulated and remain in position to facilitate their reconnection. Now release the nuts or screws securing the fire bar and carefully lift it out.

When renewing elements polish the reflectors or wash them with soap and water so that they radiate the maximum heat. Also remove dust and foreign matter which will have collected in the body of a fire. Examine the flexible cord, especially the ends within the casing. Renew an old or worn flex, making sure you know the connections for the new core colours.

Convector fires

Since the elements of convector fires operate at 'black' heat and therefore at comparatively low temperature they rarely fail or give trouble. When fitted with an illuminating device the lamp will need replacing but this is usually readily accessible. At the same time inspect the inside of the heater for foreign matter; convectors tend to draw in a lot of dust and fluff and this should be removed periodically. If the thermostat of a thermostatically controlled convector fails it will almost certainly have to be renewed, and this is often a job for the expert.

Fan heaters, which are forced convectors, also need expert attention as the interior is complicated and hardly two models are identical.

Fuel effect heaters

Lamp failure is the most common fault. They are either the 2-pin type or have ordinary bc lamp caps. Access to a lamp is usually through the back panel of the fire and sometimes through the side or front. Replace a faulty lamp by one of the same type, wattage and colour. Take care how you remove the spinner or 'flicker' assembly for this is easily bent or misaligned. This and the collection of dust deposit are the principal reasons why spinners fail. Many modern electric fires have sophisticated fuel effect devices, some of them motorised. Adjustment or repair of these is best left to the expert.

Electric irons

There are two principal types of electric iron: the standard iron, and the automatic thermostatically controlled iron in dry and steam versions. The standard iron is fitted with a removable flex connector which plugs into two pins behind the back of the handle. The metalwork is earthed by means of spring contacts on the flex connector which make a rubbing contact with the connector shield surrounding the pins on the body of the iron.

Common faults are: burnt out element; badly fitting flex connector; poor earth contacts; damaged or worn flex.

Fitting a new element

Elements are made in a wide range of types and electrical loadings and they are not interchangeable between different makes and models of irons. It is usually wise to remove the old element first to make sure that the new element is suitable. A universal element is available and will fit a number of models for it has slots instead of holes for the fixing studs.

Non-automatic iron

Remove the two domed nuts to release the handle; lift up the metal cover plate and remove the terminal screws beneath the contact pins to release the element contact strips. Remove the two hexagonal nuts holding down the cast-iron pressure plate, asbestos pad, and finally the element, which makes direct contact with the sole plate and is usually the source of the fault.

Clean the sole plate surface using fine glass paper. Place the

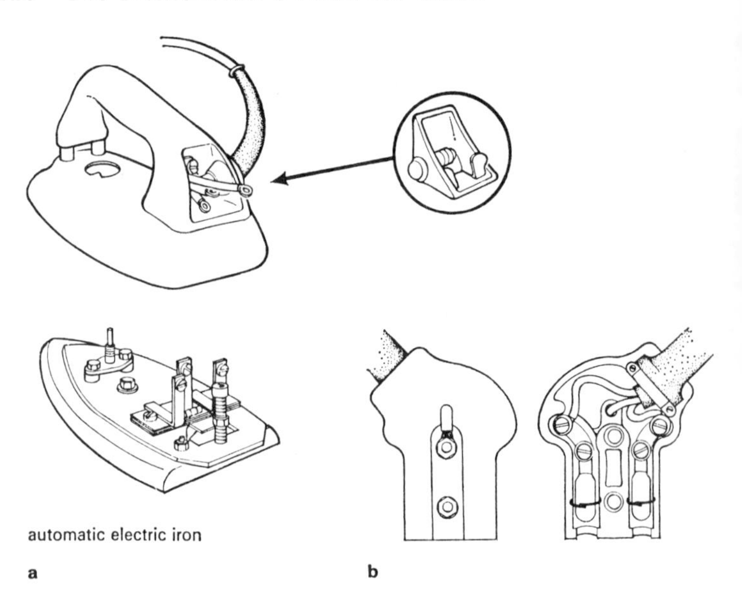

Fig. 34 (a) Flex connections of automatic iron (b) flex connector of non-automatic iron

new element in position and refit the asbestos pad and pressure plate and finally the two hexagonal nuts. These nuts must be tightened as far as they will go to keep the element flat on the sole plate surface. Position the element contact strips so that they will not foul the pressure plate or cover plate and then connect them to the pin terminals. Finally replace the cover plate and handle, and secure them with the two domed nuts.

If the connector is in a poor condition, replace it and fit a new 3-core unkinkable flex instead of the braided type you probably had originally on the iron.

Automatic electric iron

The flex of an automatic thermostatically controlled iron is connected direct to the terminals with no removable connector. It passes into the iron via a rubber or spring grommet, and access to the terminals is obtained by removing a terminal cover, usually at the rear. The terminals are colour-coded to ensure that the thermostat is in the live pole.

Common faults in addition to element failure are: maladjustment of the thermostat, which usually means the numbers on the dial do not correspond with the temperature of the sole plate; and failure of the pilot light.

The thermostat is adjustable, but this should not be attempted by the user: only a mechanic with the aid of the maker's servicing manual can do this. The householder can rarely do more than change the flex of an automatic iron. The element of some models is embedded in the sole plate, and when it fails the complete sole plate must be renewed.

A steam iron is similar to the conventional automatic 'dry' iron to repair. If tap water has been used instead of distilled water the vessel must be flushed out occasionally with a solution bought from an electrical shop or from the Electricity Board showrooms.

Electric kettles

Modern electric kettles have an immersion element which is easy to fit, but as there are numerous shapes and sizes and models of kettles it is essential that you buy the correct replacement element when yours fails.

One variation in addition to shape and type is the diameter of the element flange hole in the kettle body. Two diameters, 1 9/16 in. (40 mm) and 1 11/16 in. (43 mm), fit the majority of standard or conventional-shape kettles, but it is usually best to ask first for the same type of element as originally supplied by the makers of your kettle. If this is not readily available you can buy a standard replacement element, pre-packed complete with element washers and with or without a new length of flex and connector. One element maker, Backer Electric Ltd, has introduced a special washer which enables a 1 9/16 in. element to be fitted into a 1 11/16 in. kettle orifice.

A 1kW or 1.5kW standard ordinary-speed kettle can be converted into a modern high-speed kettle with a pre-packed conversion kit containing a 2750 watt high-speed element, locking collar, 3-pin connector and a 4 ft length of 3-core kettle flex.

The latest innovation is the automatic kettle which switches itself off when boiling. This element can be fitted to many existing kettles and replaces the former safety device which ejected the flex connector and therefore switched off the current to the kettle as it boiled dry. In practice these ejectors do not always operate and have resulted in damage to kettle, connector and flex, and in some cases have resulted in serious fires. The thermostat of the new automatic device is reset manually.

Replacing an element

Remove the connector and unscrew the collar or connector shield from the end of the element which secures it to the kettle. Remove the element by lifting it out through the kettle body. Scrape off the pieces of old washer around the flange hole, inside and outside the kettle. Fit the new rubber washer over the flange of the new element and put the element back into the kettle, making sure it is the right way up. Fit the fibre washer on the flange outside the kettle and screw on the connector shroud or collar. Tighten the flange collar using a wrench if necessary, but take care not to damage the chrome plating. When tightening, hold the element level in the kettle so that one edge is not in contact with the kettle base.

A new element usually requires a new flex connector, even where the existing one fits; but buy it with the element either separately or in a kit.

Electric toasters

There are two types of toasters: the standard non-automatic, in which a slice of bread is toasted on one side and changed over by hand; and the automatic toaster.

Element and flex failure are the two most common faults which occur with the non-automatic toaster, plus mechanical faults such as a weak or broken spring in the toast-retaining component. Elements are easily obtained for most models and are also easily fitted by removing two or more screws.

A common fault with the automatic toaster, apart from element burn-out, is the failure of the toast 'pop-up' mechanism. This device operates by means of a bi-metal strip or heat sensing device in conjunction with a solenoid, which is a form of electro-magnet. The bread, usually two slices, is placed in the racks and passed into the toaster body by pressing a lever which loads a spring. The rack is locked in position and the elements are switched into circuit. The degree of browning required is selected by adjusting a control, and when the bread is toasted the heat-sensing device unlocks and releases the spring and the toast 'pops-up'.

This is an intricate mechanism and must be serviced by the expert. It is unwise for the householder to attempt to replace a burnt-out element, for this means dismantling the toaster which can upset the 'pop-up' mechanism.

Electric cookers

The free-standing family cooker is a comparatively simple piece of equipment, though modern controls which provide automatic cooking have made it much more complicated. Apart from these controls, which are usually grouped on a panel, all the conventional cooker comprises is an oven, two or more hotplates and a grill.

The oven is thermostatically controlled, and the hotplates and grill are controlled by variable switches. The hotplate elements, grill and oven are usually mineral insulated metal sheathed, have long life and rarely give trouble. Hotplates are made in a few standard diameters and are often interchangeable between makes. They are easily removed for replacement when they fail for they usually plug into sockets or are attached by a couple of screws. Grills too are made in various sizes and these plug into sockets. Like the hotplates they can be removed by lifting the hinged hob. Oven elements, usually one each side, also plug in and are removed by first taking out the vessel racks and side panels. An electric cooker can in fact be almost completely dismantled, including the door, which can be removed for periodic cleaning.

When an oven will not heat up or gets too hot the fault will usually lie in the thermostat, unless it is an automatic cooker and the controls have not been properly set or are inoperative. In either event, servicing is a job for the expert. The variable control of the hotplates and grill is a special unit operating on a thermo-time basis. A partial failure may mean an adjustment of the control by the expert, but complete failure means a new control. Some grills and also some hotplates are controlled by 3-heat switches giving a choice of 'high', 'medium' and 'low' heat plus an 'off' position. The automatic controls, which include a clock and timer, should not be tampered with. It is, however, usually possible to replace a fluorescent tube in the panel, where fitted, but these have a long life and rarely need attention.

Table cookers

These cover a wide variety and range from a single hotplate to a 'baby' version of a free-standing cooker. None have a loading in excess of 3kW and all are fitted with flexible cords which are plugged into the standard 13A (or 15A) socket-outlet.

Flex renewal and element replacement are the principal servicing jobs which can often be undertaken by the householder. The more complicated units should be left to the expert.

Electric blankets and bed-warmers

The electric blanket is among the most useful electrical 'appliances' in the home. They are made in a wide range of single- and double-bed sizes and types. The two principal types are under-blankets and over-blankets.

The over-blanket usually has a higher wattage loading and can be controlled by an automatic device which maintains it at a constant temperature even with a varying room temperature. Others have thermostats sewn into the blanket to switch off the current should a fault arise and produce a hot spot. The elements of some have a single wire operating in conjunction with the automatic controller to cut off the currents should a fault develop. This type of blanket is placed under the overlay, usually between other blankets, and may remain switched on all night even when the bed is occupied.

Most blankets operate at mains voltage, but there is a range of low voltage blankets which operate through a mains transformer to eliminate any likelihood of electric shock. They are supplied from plug and socket-outlets which can be 13A socket-outlets with a 3A fused plug. It is *essential*, in the interests of safety, that electric blankets are fixed and used strictly in accordance with the makers' instructions; and that they are used with great care. *Never fix a blanket with any kind of pin!* Rucking or folding can damage the warming wires and lead to faults and possible fire. You should inspect a blanket and periodically return it to the makers for servicing every two years. If damaged or if water has been spilt on it, do not use it until it has been serviced.

Some thousands of fires arise each year from electric blankets, and although this may be regarded as a small amount in proportion to the millions of blankets in use, most could have been avoided if the blankets had been used or serviced correctly. Poor quality is also a cause of accidents, but it is now an offence for a shop to sell an electric blanket which does not bear the BS Kite mark denoting its approved design and quality.

Bed-warmers

A bed-warmer is a metal-cased unit similar to an old-fashioned warming pan but with a short handle. It contains one or more electric light bulbs as the heat source. It is fairly low-priced, and gives little or no trouble except for occasional lamp failure. It is used to pre-warm a bed as was the old-fashioned bed-warmer. One unit can serve one or more beds.

Power-operated domestic appliances

These appliances are those powered by an electric motor, and they cover a very wide range from clocks and shavers to refrigerators and freezers. The only difference between them and non-powered appliances, from the servicing angle, is that they contain an electric motor. Otherwise, even flex replacement is the same. Some appliances require more attention than others depending on the type of electric motor.

There are two principal types of motor fitted to domestic appliances: the universal series wound commutator motor; and the induction motor.

The first type is the one likely to cause more trouble because it is fitted with carbon brushes. Appliances commonly used in the home powered this way are vacuum cleaners and polishers, electric drills or power tools, as they are often termed, hair driers and hedge trimmers, sewing machines and mixers.

Induction motors are fitted to the larger appliances such as washing machines and refrigerators. These are very robust, have no brushes, and give no trouble over long periods: often, indeed, the lifetime of the appliance. There is, however, a small type of induction motor, termed a *shaded-pole motor*, which is fitted to extractor fans, fan heaters, small food mixers, some hair driers and numerous other small appliances including the motorised unit of fuel effect electric fires. It has no brushes, requires little or no attention throughout its lifetime and has the advantage of being a variable-speed motor, whereas the ordinary induction motor is only single-speed.

Commutator motors are also variable-speed machines and are used in conjunction with the electronic, thyristor, speed reducing control which is similar to the dimmer light switch.

Vacuum cleaners and floor polishers

The vacuum cleaner is among the most frequently used domestic appliance powered by a commutator motor. Electrical repairs which can be done by the householder are: fitting new brushes; fitting a new flex; and attending to the switch. Belt renewal of the upright type of cleaner is also a periodic repair.

Of the two types of vacuum cleaner the upright one has more moving parts and requires more attention. The following is the sequence for fitting new brushes to the motor, which should be done when the existing brushes are worn down to less than ⅜ in.:

Buy correct replacement brushes.
Locate and remove brush caps.
Lift out old brushes and check that no particles are left in the brush holder.
Place new brush in each tube and check for ease of movement.
Slightly sandpaper a sticking brush.
Depress springs and re-fit the caps.
Brushes of polishers are similarly fitted.

When fitting new brushes to a cylinder-type cleaner it is necessary first to remove the power unit. To do this you must take off the end cover from the cleaner.

Electric motors of vacuum cleaners sometimes burn out. This may be due to old age but is often because the moving parts of the cleaner become clogged with cottons, threads and other matter which stall or partially stall the motor, overload it and burn out the windings. Sometimes the armature (the rotating unit) burns out; sometimes the field coils (the stationary unit) burns out; sometimes both burn out. Replacement armatures and field coils can be bought on an exchange basis and fitted by the householder, or the complete machine can be taken to a local dealer. Premature failures can be prevented by keeping the cleaner free of dirt and emptying the dust bag each time the machine is used.

Refrigerators and deep freezers

There are two types of refrigerator. One is the compressor type powered by an electric motor; the other is the absorption type, which contains a small electric heating element.

Some versions of the absorption-type refrigerator use a gas or oil heating element in which the heater evaporises the refrigerant. The compressor type evaporises the refrigerant by compressing it.

Refrigerators operate for many years without trouble if defrosted weekly (unless automatic). The motor and compressor of this type are contained in a sealed unit guaranteed for five years; any subsequent servicing must be done by a competent mechanic using special tools and gauges. The heating element of the absorption type is replaceable.

The advantage of the absorption-type refrigerator is that it is completely silent, but the compressor type is cheaper to run, consuming less electricity per 24 hours*—but both are equally effective.

Deep freezers too have sealed units and should not be tampered with. They need de-frosting periodically.

Washing machines and spin driers

Washing machines, spin driers and twin-tub machines cover a wide range of models. Some are fully automatic, some are semi-automatic, others are manual. The automatic and semi-automatic have intricate controls and must be serviced by the trained

* *Author's note.* This no doubt appears contradictory, but the absorption type is made in the smaller sizes only and uses current for longer in a 24-hour cycle.

mechanic. Even replacing a belt on a spin drier can be complicated: it requires partial dismantling of the machine and is beyond the capabilities of the householder.

Food mixers

Both table and hand mixers have variable speeds. They are usually powered by a shaded pole induction motor. These give little or no trouble when treated with reasonable care. Flexes should be examined periodically for signs of wear or damage and the brushes of commutator motors occasionally need attention. If a mixer appears to have lost some of its power the servicing agent should be consulted.

Hair driers

A hair drier operates on a similar principle to that of a fan heater: the motor drives a fan which passes air over an electric element which it expels through a nozzle. The heater cannot be switched into circuit until the fan is first switched on. If the motor fails to operate the heater will work, but it is usually automatically switched off by a thermal cut-out before damage is caused to the appliance by excessive heat. The fan can be operated without the heater to provide cool air when required. The element is replaceable, and with some models this is easy to do by simply removing the nozzle and releasing the screws. Under no circumstances may a hair drier or other portable mains appliance be used in the bathroom, except a shaver from a socket incorporating an isolating transformer.

Mains electric clocks

Apart from occasional oiling and possibly dusting, the mains electric clock requires little attention. It has a conventional train of gears driven by a synchronous motor running at constant speed which is directly related to the speed of the generators at the power station. This enables power station engineers to keep clocks running at the right speed so they keep the correct time (provided the clock has been set at the right time when switched into circuit). Only during peak hours when power stations have had to shed some of their load by reducing the speed of the generators do clocks run slow. When the crisis is over the generators are speeded up to bring the clocks back to the correct time. Therefore, when your clock runs slow because of load shedding you should not attempt to alter it but wait until the correct time is restored by the electricity authorities.

Electric sewing machines

Electric sewing machines cover a wide variety of models, ranging from the conventional one powered by an electric motor to highly sophisticated machines in which everything is done electrically. Hand-operated or a treadle foot-operated sewing machine can easily be converted by fitting a power unit.

Power units are available to fit almost every hand- or foot-operated model. A complete kit includes a foot controller to provide variable speeds during sewing, and can incorporate a light for easier threading. It is a commutator brush machine which requires the same attention as other appliances powered by this type of motor.

Waste disposers

A waste disposer, which is a kind of mill, fitted beneath the sink waste outlet and plumbed to the waste pipe, pulverises remains of food and other kitchen refuse and washes them down the drain.

The sink waste hole has to be extra large (3½ in.) to accept the disposer. Some metal unit sinks' 1½ in. outlets can be enlarged to take the disposer connection but porcelain sinks cannot be modified. The waste disposer can be powered from a fused outlet, and can include controls which are fitted in a convenient position for the housewife.

Extractor fans

The extractor fan is designed to expel stale and moist air from a room and to remove cooking smells from the kitchen. It is suitable for most rooms but especially so in the kitchen and bathroom, where moisture causes condensation.

Fans are made in a range of types and sizes; the one most popular in the home is the type which fits in a hole cut in a pane of window glass. Sizes go by blade diameter, which determines the rate of air extraction in a given period. Speed of fan is also important, because the higher it is the more air is extracted.

A suitable size for the average kitchen is 6 in. blade diameter with a speed of 1000–2000 rpm, but fans with blade diameters of 7 in. and 8 in. are also installed. Makers always specify the rate of air extraction and from this can be worked out the number of air changes per hour which the fan will provide, i.e. about twelve changes per hour in the kitchen and about twenty per hour in the bathroom. A window fan can be mounted in a hole cut in 32 oz. (40 mm) window glass, and a glazier will cut this, but at the customer's risk. Except for very large panes it is best to replace the existing pane with a new one which has the necessary hole cut by the glazier at the time of the purchase.

Positioning of the fan is important for the maximum circulation of air. There is a model designed for fitting into a wall: bear in mind that if a wind of more than 10 mph is blowing against that wall the fan's efficiency will be affected. Remember too that draught control of boilers can be affected by an extractor fan.

Power tools

The power tool and electric portable drill are operated by a universal series wound commutator motor of the same type as fitted to the vacuum cleaner and many other high-speed domestic electrical appliances. The chuck containing the drill or other accessory is powered through a speed reduction gear box forming part of the power unit. Some models have a second lower speed for heavy duty work. Speed variation below normal can be obtained from any portable power tool or drill by means of a transistorised electronic speed controller inserted into the flexible cord, usually at the plug end. These controllers, unlike resistance units, have the advantage of producing lower speeds without drop in torque.

Most burn-out in the motor winding is caused by overload, but the tool is easily dismantled and fitted with a replacement armature and/or field windings. The carbon brushes are also easily replaced. Periodic attention to the flexible cord is advised and the earthing connection should also be checked where relevant. Some models are double-insulated, require no earthing and are fitted with 2-core sheathed flex.

Garden tools

The most commonly used electric garden tool is the hedge trimmer, powered by a commutator brush motor similar to that of the portable drill and requiring similar servicing. Double-insulated versions are preferable from the safety angle but, in common with those which need to be earthed, must be used only from sockets protected by a 30mA RCCB.

Additional safety is provided by another model, which operates at reduced voltage through a portable mains transformer.

Electric mowers

For the larger lawn a battery-powered mower is well worth while, but the battery has to be charged at the end of a short mowing session. Most low-priced mowers operating from the mains are the rotary type with the blade powered by a commutator motor. These have a thermal cut-out to reduce the likelihood of the motor burning out should the blade become obstructed in long grass or fouled by rubbish or undergrowth. The units are mainly double-insulated and are therefore fitted with 2-core sheathed flex.

Electric cylinder-type mowers in the higher price range are powered by induction motors which drive the cylinder by a belt and pulleys. Some also propel the mower, as do engine-driven machines.

Mains-powered lawn mowers must be used only from sockets protected by a 30mA RCCB.

When using either a hedge trimmer or a mower there is always the risk of cutting the flex. With the hedge trimmer, this can be avoided by throwing the flex over the left shoulder; with the mower you should lay the flex out of the run of the machine. An additional hazard, particularly with the rotary mower, is running over pebbles hidden in the long grass. These not only damage the cutting blade but are ejected from under the mower at a great force and can result in personal injury. The grass should be swept prior to mowing to prevent this.

Table 5 *Typical Loading of Domestic Appliances*

Appliance	*Loading Watts*
Bed warmer	60–100W
Blankets	50–150W
Boiling ring	750–2000W
Bottle warmer	150–180W
Car heater	300–500W
Clocks	negligible
Coffee maker	380–1200W
Coffee percolator	400–800W
Dish washer	3000W (with heater)
Fans	25–120W
Fires	
1-, 2-, and 3-bar	1000–3000W
infra-red	750–2250W
bowl	500–750W
Floor polisher	300–450W
Food mixer	100–450W
Food trolley (hostess)	200–450W
Frypan	1000–1250W
Hair drier	350–600W
Infra-red grill	1500–3000W
Iron, automatic,	750–1000W
standard type	450–500W
Jug	600W
Kettle	1000–3000W
Plate warmer	175–800W
Power-operated tools	210–260W
Radio receiver	100W

Table 5 *Continued*

Appliance	*Loading Watts*
Refrigerators	
absorption type	80–115W
compressor type	100–175W
home freezers	100–250W
Scrubbers and polishers (combined)	300–450W
Sewing machines	75W
Shaver	15W
Spin drier	100–320W
Spit (rotary)	650–2000W
Tea maker	500–750W
Television receiver	100–200W
Toaster	400–600W
Tumble drier	2500–2750W
Urn	3000W
Vacuum cleaner	220–300W
hand cleaner type	150W
Washboiler	3000W
Washing machine (unheated)	300W
Washing machine (heated)	3000W
Waste disposer	200W

14

Festive Lighting

Coloured lamps for the Christmas tree may only be used indoors. They are wired in series and are low voltage, but because they are connected to the mains supply they can give a severe shock if an exposed metal cap or filament of a broken lamp is touched by someone in the vicinity of earthed metal or a stone floor.

The voltage of each lamp depends on how many there are in a festoon. Those in a 12-lamp festoon are 20V, in a 20-lamp festoon, 12v, and in a 40-lamp festoon, 6V. It is therefore essential to replace a lamp by one of the correct voltage: this is stamped on the lamp cap.

There are two principal types of indoor festoons. One has olive or similar shape lamps or large torch-type bulbs inside decorative figures; all have mes (miniature Edison screw) lamp caps, like torches. The other type has small 'pinhead' lamps with a tiny les (lilliput Edison screw) screw cap, originally of Continental design. These are in 20- and 40-lamp festoons.

As they are wired in series, when one lamp is missing none works. When the mes type fails, one dud lamp puts the whole festoon out of action until it is replaced. When a 'pinhead' type of lamp fails, a shorting device in it maintains the current in the circuit and all the rest remain alight. But this means that the same mains voltage is now applied to fewer lamps in the series, so the voltage at each becomes higher and the lamps are 'over-run'. Other lamps consequently fail and within a short period the whole string will fail. To avoid this chain reaction it is essential to replace a 'pinhead' lamp immediately it goes out.

When a conventional mes lamp fails and the whole festoon goes out it is difficult to locate the dud, especially on a Christmas tree amongst the other decorations and presents. One method is to replace each lamp in turn with a new one, first making sure that each lamp is secure and making contact in its lampholder. A better method is to test each lamp in turn with a 6-volt battery.

Lamp life can be increased by inserting a mains voltage coloured lamp into the festoon, or increased almost indefinitely by connecting two identical festoons in series. The lamps will lose some of their sparkle but will be more reliable.

Some festoons include a flasher lamp: if not, one can be wired into the circuit unless they interfere with TV or radio reception.

The total load (wattage) of a festoon is much higher than generally realised, and it can easily overload a lighting circuit. It is better therefore to supply it from 13A ring circuit plugs and sockets with 3A fuses fitted to the plugs.

Outdoor decorations

Festoons made especially for outdoor use are weatherproof. The lamps are mains-operated coloured bulbs, either of conventional shape or 'specials'.

Lampholders are moulded into the plastic sheath of the cable to exclude moisture. There is also a press-pin type which is fitted to rubber sheathed twin-core cable. When the two sections of the lampholder are secured together on the cable the pins make contact with the stranded conductors of the cable. These festoons are widely used in municipal illumination schemes, but in the home they must be used with care, and the lampholders, once fixed, should remain in the one position. Should a lampholder be removed, moisture and rain may penetrate the pin holes through to the conductor and result in current leakage and possible shock.

Outdoor festoons can be run off garden socket-outlets or from the house using circular pvc sheathed flexible cord. The socket must be protected by a 30mA RCCB.

15

Safety in Home Electrics

Correct wiring, high quality appliances and their careful use with regular servicing are important factors for safety in home electrics. This applies to the whole installation but there are special situations where extra precautions are necessary. One is in the bathroom. The requirements here are as follows:

1. No socket-outlet may be installed in the bathroom or shower room. No mains-operated portable electrical appliance may be taken into or used in the bathroom, with one exception, an electric shaver operated from a shaver supply unit to British Standard BS3052.

This type of socket unit contains a double-wound isolating transformer, plus a thermal cut-out to prevent any appliance other than the low-current shaver being plugged into it. The supply at the socket is at mains voltage, but the output is isolated from the earthed mains to prevent shock to a person using the shaver who might touch an exposed contact when he is in contact with earthed metal.

2. No switch must be fixed within reach of someone using the bath or shower, except the insulated cord of a cord-operated ceiling switch. The alternative to a ceiling switch is one fixed on the wall immediately outside the bathroom door.

3. A light fitting in the bathroom should be totally enclosed. If an open lampholder, such as a batten lampholder, is fixed to the ceiling it must have a HO (Home Office) skirt to shield the metal cap of the bulb so that it cannot be touched when it is being taken out. A flexible cord pendant should not be installed in the bathroom.

4. A shaving mirror light, usually a striplight, must be made so that the metal lamp caps cannot be touched even when replacing the lamp. Mirror lighting units containing a shaver socket must be designed specially for bathroom use, with the shaver socket supplied from a double-wound transformer complying with BS3052. The light switch must be out of reach

of a person using the bath, and it should therefore be operated by a cord.

5. Where the hot water tank cupboard opens on to the bathroom the immersion heater must not be supplied from a plug and socket, but from a switch placed well out of reach of a person using the bath.

6. Exposed metalwork in the bathroom should be bonded (see Bonding).

Other safety precautions

As detailed in this book elsewhere, electrical appliances must be kept in good order and used properly. Wiring and accessories which become loose or damaged must be attended to without delay. Correct fuses must be used to replace blown ones and the fault which caused the fuse to blow must be located and rectified.

One very important safety factor is to unplug portable appliances when they are not being used. This particularly applies to radiant electric fires which might be placed up against furniture or other inflammable material which, if the plug were inadvertently switched on, would result in a very serious fire; and power-operated appliances, especially food mixers, which if left on the kitchen table or work area would be a danger to young children. If the power tool, hedge trimmer or mower is left unattended for a while, *pull out the plug*. Also, where there are young children, make a habit of turning off the cooker control switch when you are not using it. This will stop the clock, if one is fitted, but it will also prevent accidents where children can meddle with low-level switches.

If you change from a standard kettle to a high-speed one stay beside it during the few minutes it takes to boil. No doubt the automatic device will operate, but there is no point in leaving a kettle to boil dry while you answer the door or are engaged on the phone.

Some safety *don'ts*

Don't patch up frayed flex with insulation tape, but renew it at the first sign of wear or damage.

Don't run flex under carpets.

Don't use twin-twisted-type flex for appliances or lights.

Don't drag a vacuum cleaner or any appliance along by its flex.

Don't connect 3-core flex to a 2-pin plug.

Don't use 2-core flex for appliances except those of the double-insulated type marked with a double square.

Don't let flex droop over a radiant fire or over a cooker hotplate.

Don't wrap the flex around an iron while the iron is still hot.

Don't plug a number of appliances into a socket-outlet by means of multi-plug adaptors. Apart from a risk of overloading the socket this practice usually means long trailing flexes.

Don't have unnecessarily long flexes; keep them as short as possible by installing extra sockets.

Don't have too short a flex on an iron or kettle where this would place undue strain on the flex and may prevent the appliance being used with safety.

Don't connect more than one flex to a ceiling rose designed to take only one.

Don't run an appliance from a light fitting using a lampholder adaptor.

Don't renew a bulb without first switching off the light.

Don't stand a radiant electric fire against furniture or fabric, or face it against the wall or woodwork.

Don't stand a storage heater right against a wall unless the heater is of the recessed type.

Don't place clothes or materials to dry or air over any type of heater.

Don't let materials fall on to tubular heaters or let curtains come in contact with the tubes.

Don't have an airing cupboard heater at low level without a clothes guard.

Don't touch the element of an electric fire without first pulling out the plug or turning off the main switch, if of the built-in type not supplied from a plug and socket.

Don't dismantle a cooker for cleaning without first turning off the control switch.

Don't let cooking metal foil come into contact with elements of the open spiral wire type.

Don't use the blade of a knife or other metal object to remove bits of broken bread from a toaster, and also always first pull out the plug before attempting to clean it.

Don't use an inspection light at mains voltage when working on, or under, the car unless it's an all-insulated type of lamp with the bulb well guarded from touch should the glass break.

Don't knock nails into walls, or use drills or plugging tools to drill holes, in walls immediately above switches and socket outlets or where you suspect electric cables are buried.

Don't knock nails into floorboards which are likely to have electric cables underneath them.

16

Inspecting and Testing an Installation

The home installation should be inspected and tested periodically. A limited inspection and test may be carried out by the Electricity Board prior to the connection of an installation or of an extension, but it is often the only test made until the Board is called in again to add further wiring to the supply.

The Institution of Electrical Engineers recommends that tests should be made every five years; old installations should be tested at shorter intervals. But this is rarely done for the initiative lies with the householder. Since there are over 17 million dwellings in Britain it would be a colossal task to carry out tests frequently. An electrical contractor or the Board makes a charge for such tests.

What the householder can do

The householder can make a visual check on his electrical installation, but in the absence of the necessary instruments he is unable to make a full inspection and test as would be done by an electrical contractor.

A regular visual check should include the following items:

- switches, sockets and other wiring accessories
- plugs and flexible cords of portable appliances and table lamps
- accessible fixed wiring, including the meter tails
- earthing clamps and earthing terminals in plugs and appliances.

If considered desirable, the wiring accessories may be removed from their mounting boxes to expose the ends of conductors, but only after the main switch of the installation has been turned off. All accessories must be refitted before the supply is restored.

Testing instruments

For a full test, the instruments listed below are needed. These are expensive and are therefore not usually available to householders.

- insulation resistance tester
- continuity tester
- earth loop impedance tester
- polarity tester
- RCCB tester (if an RCCB is installed)

Insulation resistance test

This test is to check that the insulation of conductors is good, and there there will be no current leakage between conductors of different polarity or between a conductor and earth. It can only be made with an insulation resistance tester. The resistance should be not less than 1 megohm, but it will normally be about 100 megohms or more. If there is a fault such as a short circuit, or an earth fault 'of negligible impedance' caused by, say, a nail through the cable, or maybe a wrong connection, the insulation tester will indicate the fault but not where it is. Locating a fault is more difficult, and is a job for the expert.

Continuity test

This test should be applied to all circuit protective conductors and bonding conductors to ensure that they are continuous and correctly connected. If steel conduit forms all or part of the protective conductor, the test must be done with alternating current equal to 1.5 times the rating of the circuit subject to a maximum of 25A. Where all the CPCs are of copper, the test can be made using a low-current DC ohmmeter.

A similar test is made on all the conductors (phase, neutral and earth) of each ring final circuit to verify that the ring circuit is continuous. Two test methods are given in the IEE Wiring Regulations; both require accurate measurement of the resistance of the conductors. It is possible to make a visual check by removing sockets from their boxes but, in the absence of a continuity tester, it is difficult to determine if a socket having two cables is part of a ring or is the first socket of a two-socket spur which is no longer permitted.

Earth loop impedance test

This test is made at or near the main switch of the installation, usually at the nearest socket-outlet, to verify that the appropriate protective devices will operate in the event of an earth fault. A similar test can also be made at the remote end of each circuit, but an alternative method is to measure the resistances of the phase and protective conductors of each circuit and to add these to the value of the external earth loop impedance measured near the main switch; in either method, allowance has to be made for the increase of resistance which occurs under fault conditions, using the data and formulae in the IEE Wiring Regulations.

Polarity test

This test is made with a voltmeter or other voltage indicator, but not with a neon screwdriver, which can give misleading results. Its intention is to check that all single-pole switches, fuses and MCBs are in the phase conductor and not the neutral.

Since one of the two conductors of a circuit is the 'phase' and the other is the neutral, but at near earth potential, it is essential for the single-pole switch to break the current in the phase conductor, and not in the neutral.

Should the switch be inserted in the neutral conductor, turning it off would cut off the flow of current, but the terminals at a light fitting or appliance would still be live.

For example one of the pins of a lampholder would remain 'live' with the wall switch turned off. A person replacing a lamp thinking the current is off might touch the phase pin, and if this were in contact with the earth or earthed metal would receive a severe electric shock.

Where mains voltage es (Edison screw) bulbs and lampholders are fitted it is essential that the centre contact of each es lampholder is connected to the phase conductor.

Correct polarity is also important with socket-outlets. This ensures that the fuse of a plug is in the phase conductor and that appliance single-pole switches and thermostats (also single-pole) break the phase conductor. If the socket-outlet or the plug flex is incorrectly connected, the appliance switch or thermostat will not be in the phase conductor.

The polarity of a socket-outlet can be tested with a special testing plug which has a neon indicator.

If when the lighting circuit is tested all or most of the switches are in the neutral conductor, it is fairly obvious that the circuit conductors have been incorrectly connected at the fuse board or consumer unit and need changing over. If only one or perhaps two lighting switches are wrong the fault can be traced to a joint box or to a loop-in ceiling rose. To remedy it, find out which joint box or ceiling rose and change the two conductors over. The colour coding of circuit cable conductors is red for the phase and black for the neutral, but as a sheathed cable often uses black as the switch wire (which is on the 'phase' side of the circuit) the code is not an infallible guide. Where black insulated cable is used for the phase, place red plastic sleeving on the ends for identification.

The same rule can apply to socket-outlets—if all or most have reverse polarity the connections at the fuseway are reversed, but if only the odd one or so is wrong the conductors at the socket are reversed. With these circuits the colour code can be followed. *Black must be connected to black, and red to red throughout.*

What the Board inspector looks for

If a new installation wired by a contractor does not pass the Electricity Board's test, then it is the contractor, not the householder, who is responsible. In practice the contractor will make a test, and if he is approved the Board will accept his certificate without making a further test.

Where the householder has done the wiring, it should not fail the test if the information in this book is followed and the work competently carried out.

When the Board inspector examines and tests a new installation or an extension to an existing one, prior to connecting it to the mains, he has to be satisfied that the wiring and equipment are safe and that they will not interfere with other consumers' supply. He expects the installation to comply with IEE Wiring Regulations (the Regulations for Electrical Installations).

If it does, the Board is bound by statute to connect it, or the parts that do, if such a division is practicable. If the installation does not comply with the regulations in every respect, the Board has no statutory powers to withhold a connection solely on those grounds. The inspector must show that the installation would be dangerous or would interfere with the supply to others.

Refusal to connect usually means that something is seriously wrong and not just that fixing clips of cables are too widely spaced or that similar minor items do not comply. The initial test is free of charge, but a charge is made for subsequent visits.

Tests made are for the items outlined above, and how extensive these are depends, partly, on the individual inspector, for his findings benefit the Board and not the consumer. Although a consumer does gain from the knowledge that the Board has accepted the installation, he cannot regard it as a guarantee of good workmanship or hold the Board responsible if something later proves to be wrong or faulty.

Likely interference with the supply to others applies mainly to equipment; in particular to electric motors, fluorescent fittings and other inductive apparatus. Electric motors of the larger sizes are rarely installed in the home, but they are one class of apparatus where interference can be expected. The choke of fluorescent fittings is highly inductive and with most circuits causes a poor power factor which consumes wattless current not registered on the meter. A power factor correction capacitor has to be included in the circuit, but is fitted by the manufacturer and is necessary in home-constructed units built from kits of components.

When a rewire becomes necessary

An installation wired before the last war, and some in the early post-war years, employed rubber insulated and rubber or lead sheathed cable. The rubber has a limited life, not much more than 25–30 years, which means that most installations need re-wiring now (where the cable has not been disturbed, a longer life can be expected). Experience shows that most installations have, to some extent, been disturbed, if only to replace light fittings.

Pvc insulation, on the other hand, has a much longer life unless misused. As most installations are now wired in pvc insulated and sheathed cable provision for rewiring is no longer considered necessary.

The older installation

The most obvious sign of age in rubber insulated cables is that the insulation has become hard and brittle and when handled falls off the conductor, leaving it bare. This is especially so at the ends of sheathed conductors where the sheath was removed for making the connection to the switch or ceiling rose. Both the vri (vulcanised rubber insulation) and the sheath of trs (tough rubber sheath) cables are highly combustible and will start a fire where the conductor joints are poor and sparking occurs.

Cables enclosed in conduit, usually metal in the older installation, also have vri insulation but this is wrapped in tape and covered in braid (red for the phase and black for the neutral). This too is highly combustible. Conduits should terminate in metal boxes at the ceiling rose and at switches and other outlets so that the vri cables are completely enclosed in fire resistant material. In the older installation conduits usually terminate a few inches from the outlet leaving the conductors exposed and a fire risk.

Switches and accessories

The older switch, ceiling rose, light fitting, socket-outlet and other accessories usually mounted on wood blocks are now obsolete. They should be replaced by modern switches and accessories, mounted on plastic surface boxes or metal flush boxes with the sheath of the cable passing into the box. Modern ceiling roses and ceiling switches are mainly enclosed and require no mounting box.

Main switches and fuses

Where the older installation has a number of main switch and fuse units for the various circuits, instead of one composite consumer unit for all, they should be given early attention, but to replace them will involve some rewiring. Those which have double-pole fuses should be replaced by single-pole fuse or MCB units without delay. Earthing of metal lighting fittings and switches is also an urgent job. Any 2-pin plugs and socket-outlets, other than the modern shaver socket, should be replaced by 3-pin versions and a circuit protective conductor run to each one.

The modern installation

The modern installation is usually wired in pvc sheathed cable. Where wires are in high ambient temperatures, such as at the ends where they terminate in enclosed light fittings and where there is heat transferred from the lamp to the conductors, via the lampholder, the pvc is liable to melt and cause corrosion of the copper conductors. Ends of the cables where this is likely to happen should be examined and the final few inches should be covered by heat resistant sleeving or replaced by heat resistant cable with silicone rubber insulation. To effect the conversion, a joint box or special pattress box fitted with terminals is needed.

Earthing of metal light fittings and switches is also important because only the more recently wired lighting circuit will have cables embodying a circuit protective conductor.

All circuits should be checked for possible overload, especially where points have been added since the installation was first wired. Finally, any loose switches, light fittings, socket-outlets and other accessories must be securely fixed, even though this may mean removing the fitting to provide better support or re-plugging the wall to secure the pattress box. Damaged or broken accessories must be replaced without delay.

Beware of moonlighters

Because rewiring has become a priority job in the older, owner-occupier dwelling, householders in some districts are pestered by people offering to do this job at seemingly attractive prices. These self-appointed electricians are mainly unqualified and employed in other jobs during the day. Some offer a free inspection with the intention of frightening the householder into having work done whether necessary or not, as in one case where the property had only been rewired a couple of years earlier.

The prices quoted are for the bare mininum which, with the necessary 'extras', brings the final price to an exorbitant figure and does not include making good chases in plaster or relaying floor coverings. The Electricity Board or a reputable contractor* will make a test for a reasonable figure, and it is best to get quotations from the Board and from two approved contractors whose names can be obtained from the Board's offices.

These jobs carry a guarantee and extended payment terms can be arranged, but unless part of other improvements the work does not qualify for a government home improvement grant.

* Reputable contractors may be found by referring to the Roll of Approved Contractors issued by the National Inspection Council for Electrical Installation Contracting, 36/37 Albert Embankment, London SE1 7UJ.

17

Getting a Supply of Electricity

When you move house it is necessary to apply to the local Electricity Board for a supply of electricity. You can write to them, or if in the neighbourhood you can call at their showrooms.

You will receive an application form for you to give details of when you want the supply to commence, and where the Board official can get the key if you have not already moved into the premises. Details of the appliances and lamps and any special equipment including fluorescent lights which you will have connected will also have to be supplied. This information enables the Board to check that the service cable is adequate for the assumed current demand and the current rating of the meter.

If wiring work has been carried out since the last occupier vacated the premises you, or your contractor if you have employed one, will have to give details on the relevant form.

If the house has been occupied very recently the connection of the meter will be little more than a 'matter of form', and may involve no more than replacing the Board's service fuse if this has been removed. If you move in the same day or the day after the previous occupier moves out, possibly only the meter will be read without the need for temporary disconnection.

Either way the Board inspector may wish to test and inspect the installation for his own satisfaction. If it does not come up to the required standard or does not comply with the regulations the Board is unlikely to disconnect or refuse to reconnect it—its powers are limited by statute to situations which are specifically dangerous. The usual procedure is to make a 'temporary connection', which is followed by a letter detailing what is wrong and requesting that the 'faults' are rectified. (See Chapter 16.) If the house is a new one and you the first occupier, testing the installation will be the responsibility of the builder's electrician, and should there be anything wrong he will have to put it right, but not at your expense.

Service charges

If you move into a house or cottage without a mains supply of electricity and you intend having the supply to the premises, you will probably be asked by the Board to make a contribution towards the cost in the form of a service charge. The amount will depend upon the distance of the premises from the distribution cable and the position of the meter in the house.

If the distribution cable does not run along the street or lane, or if it is an overhead cable more than about 60 ft (20 m) away, the contribution you have to make can be quite high. The Board does not expect the whole cost of the service to be met by the consumer, and is usually prepared to negotiate when a load such as cooking and storage heating is installed, which provides substantial revenue. If only lighting is required the contribution is likely to be higher. Where more than one house requires a supply, much of the cost can be shared and individual contributions made smaller.

18

Paying for your Electricity

An electricity tariff is the means of charging for electricity consumed by the particular service provided. Each area Electricity Board has a number of different tariffs and the consumer has a choice. They operate on a quarterly basis and generally the more units consumed, the lower the average price per unit of the electricity used.

The most widely adopted domestic tariff is the 'two-part' tariff comprising a *standing charge* determined by the cost of having electricity available at all times and a *unit rate* for each unit consumed. The charges vary between Electricity Boards, but the average figures are £7.08 per quarter for the standing charge and 5.41 pence per unit for the unit rate (February 1987 prices).

For supplying storage heaters and off-peak water heating, the average figures for the 'Economy 7' tariff are £9.31 per quarter for the standing charge and 5.64 pence for 'day' units and 2.04 pence for 'night' units.

Only the Economy 7 tariff is now available for new off-peak installations, but older installations are still supplied on a variety of tariffs which are too numerous to list here. The Economy 7 meter ('White meter' in Scotland) has two number displays—one for the units used during the 17-hour 'day' period and the other for the lower cost units used during the 7-hour 'night' period, usually from 12.30 to 07.30 hours GMT. A time-switch, provided by the Board, selects the appropriate display and controls the operating period of the off-peak equipment.

Which tariff to choose

When you move house it is necessary to decide which tariff you intend to adopt. Unless you have electric storage heating, you will usually find that the two-part tariff is of most financial benefit. If you do not have night storage heating, the Electricity Board representative will no doubt advise against the Economy 7 tariff unless you expect to use an abnormally large amount of electricity during the cheap-rate period. You have to allow for the fixed charge and the increase in the day rate on the Economy 7 tariff before you can expect an advantage.

You can change to Economy 7 tariff at any time, but as it must run for at least a year you cannot have the advantage of it in the winter and then discard it in the summer when you are not likely to use so much electricity at night.

When you have the Economy 7 tariff you can check the consumption of the two rates by referring to the figures on your electricity bills over the year, but don't forget to add the fixed charge.

What to do about an extra-high bill

When you receive what appears to be an excessive bill for the quarter's electricity, the most likely answer is that you have in fact used the amount of electricity indicated. Try to recall whether fires were left on for exceptionally long periods during a cold spell or during an illness, or whether an immersion heater was left switched on by mistake.

Another possible reason is that previous bills were based on estimated consumption, because you were out when the meter reader called, and low estimates have now caught up with you following an actual meter reading. If you make a check of the meter reading after the amount has been estimated you will know whether a substantial bill is being 'clocked up'.

If there is no obvious solution you can consult the Board for there may be an accounting mistake.

As a final resort you can question the accuracy of the meter and possibly have a check meter installed for a period. If you are not genuinely satisfied you have the right to have the meter tested at an official testing station which comes under the jurisdiction of the Department of Trade and Industry. If this shows the meter to be accurate you will have to pay for the test. If it is inaccurate there is no charge and your bill will be adjusted, but remember the test may show that the meter is reading slow, not fast, and any adjustment of your bill might not be in your favour. Rarely is a meter found to be reading high or inaccurate for each one is tested as a statutory requirement.

To query an account does not give a consumer any rights to withhold payment for this could also be used as an excuse to delay payment of the account due.

Every householder should learn to read a meter. The 'Economy 7', or 'White', meter has digital dials which are as easy to read as the mileage on a car odometer. Meters with clock dials require experience and are not easy to read unless you know how.

For practice study the dial in Fig. 35. Ignore the small dial on the extreme right marked 1/10 kWh and read the others from left to right. Where a pointer is at a whole number and it is difficult to tell whether it has reached or passed it, check the next lower dial on the right. If the pointer of that one is between the 9 and 0 you take the lower number of the dial in question. If the pointer of the dial on the right is between the 0 and 1 you take the higher number. For example, the pointer on the first dial in Fig. 35 is at the 3, but as the pointer on the next dial is between 9 and 0 the figure to read is 2, which is a difference of 1000kWh (units). Where the pointer is between two numbers, as is usual, the correct reading is always the lower number. The meter in Fig. 35 reads 2978kWh.

Abbreviations

Ampere (unit of electric current)	A
Milliampere (= $^{1}/_{1000}$th ampere)	mA
Volt (unit of electric force)	V
Watt (unit of electric power)	W
Kilowatt (= 1000W)	kW
Kilowatt-hour (unit of electricity consumption)	kWh
Miniature circuit breaker	MCB
Residual current circuit breaker	RCCB
Circuit protective conductor	CPC

Index